Rolaboi, Revival

ROLABOi
REViVAL

2OTH ANNIVERSARY
REVISED EDITION

Written by
JAYSON SUTCLIFFE

Rolaboi, Revival

Memoir of a World Champion Roller Skater

Jayson Sutcliffe

Singular Pictures

ROLABOi
Revival
Copyright © 2024 by Jayson Sutcliffe

Published by Singular Pictures 2024
Melbourne, Australia.

All Rights Reserved

ISBN: 978-1-7636334-6-9
EISBN: 978-1-7636334-9-0

National Library of Australia listing:
Sutcliffe, J.
Rolaboi

No part of this book may be reproduced in any form, whether by photocopying or by any electronic or mechanical means, including information storage or retrieval systems, without written permission from both the copyright owner and the publisher, except in the case of brief quotations embodied in critical articles and reviews.

This book is a work of non-fiction. Due to current defamation laws, the identities of several individuals have been altered to prevent any association with Jayson from leading to potential litigation due to embarrassment. This book intends not to embarrass or expose anyone, and efforts have been made to avoid this whenever possible.

CONTENTS

DEDICATION xiii
PREFACE xiv

1 | COME INTO MY WORLD 1

2 | OBSESSION 25

3 | SECRET LIFE ON THE INSIDE 54

4 | GROWING UP OVERNIGHT 64

5 | MOVING ON 96

6 | THE BIG BREAK 126

7 | WHERE TO FROM HERE? 134

8 | THIS TIME I KNOW IT'S FOR REAL 157

9 | YOU LEFT US SO SUDDENLY 188

CONTENTS

10 | DARK HORSE FROM DOWN UNDER 202

11 | HOME AWAY FROM HOME 222

12 | THE NEW APPROACH 257

13 | PAVING THE WAY 298

14 | THE LONG ROAD TO THE TOP 319

15 | SALTARON LOS CANGUROS 335

HISTORY	377
ABOUT THE AUTHOR	379
ACKNOWLEDGEMENTS	380
CONTRIBUTIONS	382
STUDENTS	384
SUPPORT	385
PHOTOGRAPHIC CONTRIBUTIONS	386
EDITORIAL CONTRIBUTIONS	389

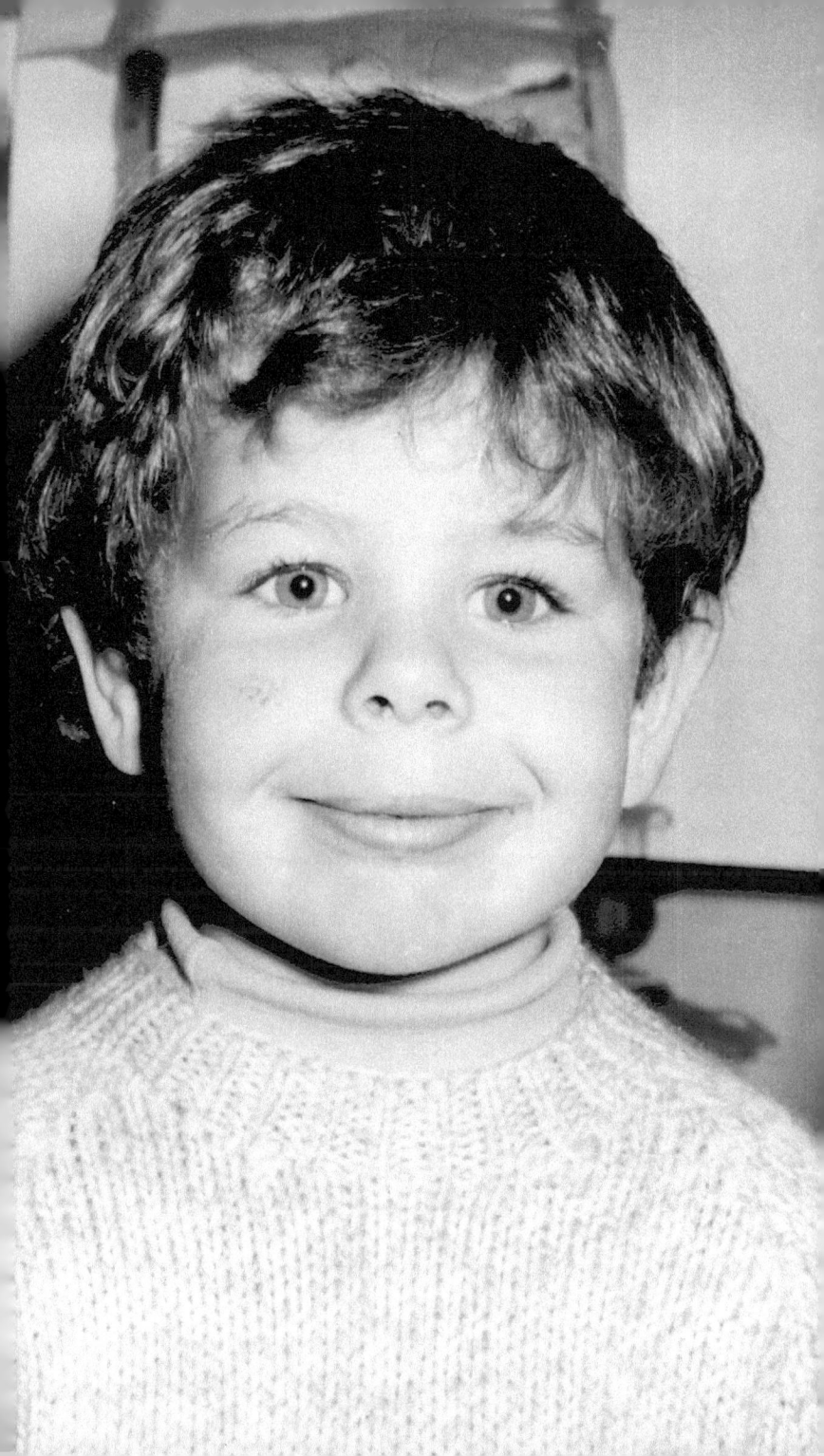

In a country that loves its sport as much as Australia, it's a travesty that Jayson Sutcliffe's achievements have not been celebrated as they should have been.

Hopefully, this honest and endearing account of his life will change that, and Sutcliffe will receive the recognition he deserves.

LUKE DENNEHY
Journalist.

As I grew up, there was no other skater more beautiful to watch than Jayson Sutcliffe, and finally, the story that took him to the top has been told.

An emotional and heartwarming journey. A story that is not only about his struggles but an inspiring story about the beauty of self-belief, dedication, and believing in dreams.

MELISSA GEORGE

THANKS

I am profoundly grateful to my loving parents, Beverley and Colin, for allowing me to grow, accepting me, and so much more.

This journey on wheels would not have been possible without you both by my side.

Your unwavering support and sacrifice have made my dream a reality.

You have given me everything,

even when I didn't ask.

R.I.P Dad

Love you both.

DEDICATION

This book is dedicated to two extraordinarily unique and exceptionally talented women who, not to mention being special, both gave and shared with me a lifelong dream...

Lynda Flint (Paulding)

and

Charmaine.

PREFACE

When my best friend gave me an autobiography as a Christmas gift in 2001, my initial thought was, "I don't really read much." But after just three chapters, I found myself eagerly typing away at a desk, recounting my life story. Publishing the work was never my intention; it was simply a way to find clarity in my life then.

Writing provided answers to many questions I had as a child and as an adult. Documenting the past is no easy task; it involves a mix of pain and passion, often feeling overwhelming and exhilarating. This process made me realize that my life hasn't been all roses. Significant highs, akin to mountain tops, and considerable lows have imparted guidance and knowledge only failure can bring.

What I've written is a candid account of my life. I wanted to celebrate my involvement in my sport, the intensity of competition, the friendships it fosters, and the memories it creates. I achieved that, but another side of my life demanded to be told—the untold stories that remained inner secrets until writing gave me the courage to confront them. I hope anyone who reads this book and has encountered similar events will find the strength to address their issues and ultimately find closure or prevent such incidents for others.

My involvement in a unique and obscure sport like artistic roller skating was never in question when I first took to wheels. It was a sport like any other and was extremely popular at the time—it was the '80s, after all. However, being different was questionable. Was I different? Who had the answers? What was so different about me? I sought to discover this and what the sport revealed—a side of me that neither my family nor I had known or experienced.

Being surrounded by creative people and the competitive skating environment gave me a dream—a goal to be the best in the world, a reason to be alive. People around me, including my family, wanted to see me achieve that goal, regardless of whether I was rebellious or different. With their support, I ultimately achieved it. I also learned that life is much more enjoyable when dreams are shared with family and friends.

Now, twenty years after the release of "Rolaboi, Renegade Skater," I've revisited my journey with a renewed perspective, delving deeper into the 'Early Years.' This reflection has brought new insights into the early struggles, triumphs, and experiences that defined the renegade spirit.

1

COME INTO MY WORLD

Long before any dreams of becoming a champion roller skater or even knowing what a wheel was, my arrival into this world was uncertain. One incredible woman, my mother Beverley, faced a grave decision. Her doctor advised her to terminate the pregnancy due to her severe illness. Yet, Beverley held steadfast to her beliefs and refused.

At twenty-seven, Beverley was no stranger to heartache. She was grappling with profound depression after the devastating loss of her six-month-old daughter, Lisa, to cot death. Her sorrow was compounded by the tragic suicide of her first husband, Neville, at their home in Warrnambool, Victoria, some years earlier, which left her alone, destitute, and overwhelmed with three young children: my brothers Tony and Colin and my sister Leanne.

Despite the heavy burden of grief, Beverley's strength and faith illuminated the path to my birth.

Enter Colin (Senior). My father didn't just appear out of nowhere; he had known my mother since they were kids. As they grew older, their tight-knit group of friends often gathered by the serene Hopkins River in Warrnambool and at the lively Saturday night dances at the local hall.

Some eight months after Neville's tragic death, Colin and his mother, my dear grandmother Jean, stepped in to support Beverley when she needed it most. It wasn't long before Colin and Beverley fell in love and married, creating a new chapter in their lives.

Dad, always as cheeky as I remember, would sneak over late at night to the tiny house my mom was renting with the kids, surprising her with gestures like flowers, ones he'd nicked from a neighbor's garden. My mom, barely managing to pay the bills with her job at the hospital, appreciated these moments of joy. She had been working at the hospital since she was thirteen, taking on tasks in the kitchen, the dorms, and anywhere else she was needed. Despite her hardships, she found solace and strength in the love and support of Colin and Jean.

On one surprise visit to Mom's home, Colin brought more than his usual charm and warmth; he brought a marriage proposal. Beverley was taken aback, but a wave of relief washed over her. The prospect of having a loving father figure for her three children in a man she cared deeply for was a blessing. They soon married at a quaint Presbyterian church in regional Terang and decided to start anew in Melbourne.

In their newly rented home in Clyde Street, Oakleigh, they conceived and welcomed baby Lisa into the world, a joy tragically cut short by her untimely death. The grief was immense, plunging Beverley into a deep depression. Yet, within a year of Lisa's passing, another life began to take shape—mine. I entered this world on May 25, 1970, a plump 7-pound baby with an insatiable cry that seemed to fill every corner of our home.

Mom's decision to continue with the pregnancy was a pivotal moment in her battle with depression. Although the darkness lingered for several years, my birth brought her a renewed sense of meaning and purpose. Tony, Leanne, and Colin Jr. were growing up fast, and the family expanded once more with the arrival of my younger brother, Shane, three years later.

Our home was a blend of chaos and love, where the sounds of children's laughter and cries intermingled with the gentle hum of daily life. Despite the shadows of the past, our family found strength in each other, carving out moments of joy and creating a new path of hope.

1971 - Bev, Jayson, Colin, Tony, Leanne & Colin Jnr.

As a child watching Saturday morning cartoons, I plunged headfirst into a world where I could be a hero, a champion, someone who defied the odds and emerged victorious. But stepping out of that imaginary realm into the intricate dance of real life, even at a young age, I felt a lingering sense of not fitting in. My older brothers, now in their teens, played baseball and often challenged me to join, but team sports and physical contact left me cold; I craved something less rowdy and more creative.

I spent countless hours sprawled on my bed, sketching my favorite cartoon heroes: Astro Boy, Marine Boy, Road

Runner, and Speed Racer. Each character mesmerized me with their distinct qualities and thrilling adventures, providing a sanctuary where my imagination could soar.

Beyond my love for cartoons, my true passion lay with horses. I adored drawing them, capturing their grace and power on paper. My fascination deepened when I developed a crush on Joanne in primary school, mainly because she had a horse and brought it to school one day. She let me ride it, and from that moment, I was hooked. I dreamed of becoming a jockey, picturing myself in the saddle, racing towards the finish line, marrying Joanne, and living on a ranch filled with horses.

Reality hit hard when I realized I'd be too tall to pursue that dream. It was a bitter pill to swallow, having my aspirations dashed by something beyond my control. But, like most kids, I quickly moved on and never married Joanne.

At nine, my interest in ballet was sparked by a curious fascination with the elegant spectacle of men in tights. Something was mesmerizing about their muscular legs and how they moved with grace and power, wearing elaborate, sequinned costumes that shimmered under the stage lights. It might have been the peculiar sight of their prominent bulging crotches or the awe of watching them perform intricate routines with such poise and strength.

Whatever it was, the combination of athleticism and artistry captivated my young imagination and drew me into the enchanting world of performance and dance.

The first time I witnessed ballet was on television, and I was instantly spellbound. The dancers glided across the stage with an effortless grace that seemed almost magical. Inspired, I began mimicking their elegant moves in the living room, twirling and leaping to the music of Don Quixote one hot summer's day in my swimwear and a t-shirt. I felt like I was part of the performance, lost in the dance's rhythm and beauty.

That is until my mom walked in. She stopped in her tracks, a look of surprise quickly turning to disapproval.

> *Don't go prancing around in here like that. Go outside and put some pants on!*

Her voice breaking the spell and bringing me back to reality. Her words stung, but the seed of my fascination with ballet had already been planted, and I knew it wouldn't be easily uprooted.

However, ballet wasn't exactly high on the family approval list, with three brothers, two of whom were heavily into baseball, cars, girls, and lifting weights. Instead, I was taken to a local park to try out for the junior baseball team. When the coach lined me up to face the ball, I swung, missed, and missed again. I was terrified. That was the extent of my baseball career. My brothers would call me 'sissy' all the time, but I quickly grew tired of it. Their efforts to force their macho image of what boys should do onto their little brother was a battle they would never win.

I wasn't particularly keen on playing soccer or football, but I eventually settled on tennis as a compromise. It wasn't a widely popular sport then, but I was intrigued by the prospect of getting a new racket, and the tennis club was conveniently nearby, so I decided to try it. I attended a weekly class for a while but wasn't showing signs of becoming the next John McEnroe or enjoying it as much as I had hoped.

Meanwhile, my sister Leanne regularly visited the local roller rink in Springvale with her high school friends Janine and Christine. She was popular with the boys—vibrant and flirtatious. My older brothers Tony and Colin often tagged along as escorts, though I suspect they enjoyed the attention, too. Muscular and dedicated to weight training, Tony was a bit of a heartthrob and popular with the girls. Smaller but still part of the group, Colin commanded respect—I wouldn't dare cross him, but he always had my back. I'd watch them strut off together from the corner of our street, wishing I could go with them.

> *We used to go to the Rink on a Friday night, and it was fantastic. The atmosphere, the music, dressing up and doing your hair, all the weird and wild makeup we used to wear—silver eyeliner was back in then! It was just fantastic... And basically, flirt a lot—a real lot! And I was really good at skating, too... LEANNE SUTCLIFFE (CHRISTIE)*

It wasn't until Christmas 1980 that I stumbled upon a pair of old strap-on roller skates by chance. We were leaving my grandma's house in Warrnambool when I spotted them in her dilapidated garage. The bearings were seized with rust from years of neglect in the damp garage. Yet, to me, they were like a pair of magic shoes. Colin helped me fit my shoes into the skates, and soon, I found myself gliding down the driveway. It was pure bliss—fumbling down the hill on those rickety skates without a care. I never wanted to take them off my feet.

I quickly pleaded with Leanne to take me to the local rink, but she hesitated to include me in her evening outings, maybe afraid I'd cramp her style. Instead, she agreed to take me on a Saturday morning to skate the public session. It was a beginning — enough to spark my passion. The mirror ball hanging from the roof, the flashing lights, pinball machines, 80s music, and skaters everywhere were heaven to me. Though the rink was small by most standards, it felt enormous, and I relished every moment. My younger brother, Shane, joined us, displaying absolute fearlessness on wheels, racing around like a Formula One driver. With him being three years younger, we were both little daredevils on wheels and were often asked to 'slow down.' The smooth concrete floor, coated with urethane, provided a vastly different experience than gliding down the driveway, where you'd often trip on pebbles and bumps in the pavement. It took several hours and numerous blisters before I began to feel comfortable and genuinely embrace the sensation under my feet. From then on, Saturday afternoons became a ritual for skating.

Coincidentally, our neighbor John Hawkins had also delved into the artistic side of the sport. Watching him skate, I realized this was as close to ballet as I might get, and I knew instantly that I wanted roller skating to consume my life.

Surprisingly, I failed physical education in high school. I felt so intimidated by other guys in my class that I'd often "forget" my uniform, except for days involving activities like trampolining or gymnastics, where I knew I could excel. In team sports, the bigger, more "macho" boys seemed to think this was a great excuse to lay into the 'slighter' guys at any chance, and I wasn't the kind to fight back.

I began taking beginners' lessons at the roller skating rink under the guidance of a spirited twenty-year-old female coach who drove a quirky Volkswagen Beetle. Her name was Lynda Flint, and she quickly became my guiding light. At eleven, I strongly desired to impress her and prove I could achieve anything she asked. Lynda fascinated me with her bold personality and unique fashion sense. I vividly remember her wearing a purple wool poncho adorned with bright yellow pom-poms paired with colorful leggings and leg warmers over her skate boots. Her blonde hair, teased and streaked with pink, completed her striking look. I was utterly captivated and determined to earn her full attention by outshining the seasoned skaters vying for the spotlight at the rink. If that was the challenge, I was ready to take it on.

> *When Jayson came into my life at Rollerworld, I was in the middle of giving a lesson to a student. As I demonstrated a move, I noticed a little kid with blue and yellow toy roller skates trailing behind us, mimicking everything I was teaching. Intrigued, I turned around and said, "Hello there, would you like to join in?" His eyes lit up, and he nodded enthusiastically, "Yes."*
>
> *It didn't take long for the parents of some of my students to notice Jayson's potential. They approached his lovely parents, Colin and Bev, and convinced them to let him have private lessons...*
> LYNDA FLINT (PAULDING).

Before long, Lynda noticed my quiet progress on wheels. She promptly encouraged me to join the advanced class, a significant step for me—and anyone else joining—considering how intimidated I felt by the other skaters. They all had expensive skates and club tracksuits, knew each other well, and naturally seemed more skilled than me. But I wasn't about to be deterred! I had a teenage crush on Lynda. Some days, she'd arrive at the rink in her boyfriend's white TR7, and I'd imagine what it would be like to date her. Sometimes, I'd arrive early before class to wait outside for her. When I greeted her, I knew she'd let me sit in the car while she unpacked her gear. With a cigarette in hand, she greeted me with a big smile and a friendly "Hi-ya, Jayse." I dreamed about driving away with her in that car and owning a rink where she'd teach me all day, just the two of us.

Skating quickly became a daily routine for me. Even in primary school, I would eagerly pedal my bike to the rink after classes for training and lessons. My skates were packed into a bag slung over my handlebars, with the wheels peeking out from the top. I'd often gaze at them as I rode along. As my commitment to roller sports deepened, so did the need for financial backing. What began as a hobby became a serious pursuit, requiring new equipment and extra lessons. I had started surpassing the regular classes, and it was time to consider private lessons. However, it was a significant commitment at $4 for fifteen minutes! My parents sacrificed to support my dedication, ensuring I had everything I needed while providing for four other siblings. It wasn't easy for them. I can never fully convey my gratitude or repay them for their steadfast encouragement and support, particularly since skating, despite its challenges, seldom offers substantial financial rewards for excellence.

> *I remember one day I was in the backyard, and you'd been at the rink in Springvale for your regular Saturday afternoon skate, and a lady, Pam Prosser, came down the driveway of the house and said, "We've been watching Jayson roller skating, and we'd like him to come and join the club and be coached by Lynda Flint." That was when we knew he was serious...* COLIN SUTCLIFFE (DAD)

Every skater dreamed of having the best equipment available, and I was no exception. However, in those days, paying over $300 for a pair of roller skates was considered absurd and beyond reach for most. My first pair was a funky blue and yellow suede style with a 'disco-inspired' design, bought from a toy store in Oakleigh for $49.00—a price my mom scoffed at, little knowing what was to come. Looking back, they'd be considered pretty cool and almost on-trend.

My neighbor and good friend John had the ultimate Snyder skates, which were pure gold to me. They had shiny silver frames with black leather boots, and the wheels seemed to spin forever. I envied him greatly. Through John, I discovered opportunities to compete at state, national, and even international levels, which only fueled my envy. While he was off jetting around the country, I was stuck at home, yearning for my adventures. Suddenly, I had my first real goal: to achieve my childhood dream of becoming a world champion!

'Don't go prancing around in here like that.'

2

OBSESSION

If my sister Leanne had taken me to an ice skating rink instead of a roller skating rink, my story might be entirely different—almost unbelievably so! And she took me on plenty of adventures, like riding on the back of a motorbike on my cousin's farm; she was fearless. The support and recognition that ice skating receives are remarkable and well-deserved, but let's be frank, roller skating is like Go-Karting is to Formula 1; it just doesn't get the attention or recognition in Australia that ice does, and you could say in many countries around the world. I hope that artistic roller skating can achieve such heights one day, too. There was a moment of great hope in '82 when a newspaper article featuring my then idol, local skater Simon Reeves, suggested that artistic skating might feature in the '84 Olympics. That was a massive motivation for us, even though our sport hasn't yet reached that goal, and it isn't getting any easier as it becomes increasingly more difficult for sports to be included in the Olympics for various reasons.

As a teenager, I used to sit in the school library, not because I loved books, but more often to avoid being bashed on the oval by dickheads, or the threat of my head being 'flushed' in the toilet because I was a 'faggot.' So, I used to roam the aisles and consistently check out the same book to gaze at it. It wasn't about roller skating like I wanted, but about ice skating, with Robin Cousins on the cover. He wore a red costume with three white stripes down the arms and legs, resembling an Adidas tracksuit. It was the most fantastic costume I had ever seen, and I yearned to have one just like it. Robin Cousins remains one of my all-time heroes—a true master of the sport and a genuine artist. Not only was he an Olympic champion, but he also captivated audiences with his charisma. As a teenager, I admired him even more for being the first to perform the 'layout backflip' on ice, instantly earning him 'cool' status.

In 1981, I eagerly attended a roller competition to experience it firsthand. That year, the National Championships took place in Melbourne at Skateworld, Noble Park, where I witnessed the Juvenile Boys division, John, competing. The atmosphere was beyond anything I had ever known. It was electric, pulsing with anticipation, nerves, and fierce competition. I could feel the excitement coursing through my veins as I took in the sea of enthusiastic spectators and skilled skaters in their team uniforms. It was the first time I realized what I'd missed out on.

My mother seemed to understand my unwavering determination to skate, so she devoted her full attention to supporting me. In hindsight, this may have strained the rest of the family, but I must acknowledge that my mom played a crucial role in my skating journey. Sometimes, it felt like I was receiving special treatment to pursue my dream, yet looking back, my brothers and sisters appeared willing to sacrifice so I could go the extra mile. But, yes, there were plenty of times when it wasn't so simple, too, and I'd often find myself in screaming matches with my siblings, and often my parents, over mindless things that related to my obsession with skating, not having something, or not getting my way. I admit I was difficult, and it must have been nightmarish for my family.

> *I think the bond between Mom and Jayson has been since he was a child, and she was so supportive of him in everything.*
>
> *Jayson was always getting the attention, the little brat! I'm not sure why it was, but he's always been a special child, and I reckon it did annoy me when I was young, but I didn't really think about it because I knew that he wanted to skate, that's all he wanted to do, skate, prance around the house make his costumes.*
>
> *Everything was Jayson at the house, but I didn't get into trouble as much because of it! ...*
> LEANNE SUTCLIFFE (CHRISTIE)

Despite my dad's constant reminders about the importance of education in securing a solid future, my passion for skating always took precedence. Dad was a woodwork teacher at Caulfield Secondary College, a good one at that. He loved making things with his hands and extended his knowledge in a way that reminded me so much of my coach, Lynda. I often wondered why my brothers had been expelled from Dad's school and what might happen if I attended the same one. Fortunately, I didn't; it was more than thirty minutes from home. Instead, I went to a nearby high school to minimize travel time home to get to my afternoon training sessions. I couldn't devote the same time to studying as I did to training, especially since I often didn't get home from the rink until eight o'clock at night. Exhausted, homework was the last thing I wanted to do, and I rarely did it.

Less than a year later, I was preparing for my first National Championships, which almost didn't happen. Our beloved 'Rollerworld' suddenly closed, and when Lynda broke the news to me, I bawled like a baby for days. I feared not knowing where I would skate or if I would continue at all. Fortunately, we found a new place: 'Roller City Frankston.' My initial thought was, 'Oh my god, Frankston? That is so far away, I'll never be allowed to go there.' However, my parents gave in to my sobbing and begging. Before we knew it, we made the daily pilgrimage down the motorway to Frankston. This had a huge impact on the family. Mom would take me, then come home to cook dinner. Dad would get home from work and rush down to pick me up at 7 or 8 pm. But the best thing about Roller City was the skaters! There were numerous talented skaters and coaches, and the rink was enormous. I loved it. It didn't take long to make new friends, and soon enough, I became best friends with Blair Withers, Sam Peake, Tim Newman, Ingrid Gossel, and Trish Darcy.

One of the best female skaters in Melbourne, Jenny Downard, who had represented Australia at the previous World Championships and was known for her exceptional spins and performances, trained there on Mondays. She was my first skater-girl crush, aside from Lynda. Jenny was tiny but could skate her heart out. She fired me up, inspired me to skate as I'd never skated before, and helped me with the inverted camel spin, a move typically not done by males at the time, although today, many include it in their routines. The inverted camel soon became my trademark spin, something I owe to Jenny.

> "Jayson used to write me 'fan' love letters and give them to me weekly, so I happily let him copy my spins, and I'd help him until he started getting a lot better!..."
> JENNY DOWNARD (COXHILL)

Making the state team was unbelievable, and the thought of traveling for skating—especially since I'd never been beyond Warrnambool—felt surreal. Heading to Newcastle in New South Wales felt like going overseas. A convoy of three cars from the Rollerworld Springvale Club journeyed up the coast together, which, looking back, probably resembled something out of 'The Adventures of Priscilla.' Our group traveled in four cars, making plenty of stops to refuel, stretch, and switch vehicles. Any opportunity to travel with Lynda was a thrill for me. It was also the first time I wore my Victorian team tracksuit, and I don't think I took it off all week.

Initially, I entered the National Championship for the experience, to try my hand, and to gauge the competition from interstate skaters. Following the state meet, I was ranked third among males in my division from a modest field of four. Leading up to the competition, all eyes were on Neale Warr from Queensland, the favorite to win after claiming the National title the previous year. The thought of competing against him and ten other boys sent a shiver down my spine. However, I was in for a big surprise when I finally met him during our first unofficial training session at the Bennetts Green Skating Rink. He was training with Queensland skaters before our private time, and I shrieked like a little girl when I heard he was inside on the rink.

No disrespect to Neale, but as it turned out, while he was still a great skater, he wasn't quite the skater I had built him up to be, given that I had pictured him somewhere between Superman and Rudolph Nureyev; it shouldn't have been that much of a shock. As soon as I learned he was not, in fact, endowed with superpowers, my confidence accelerated to a level I wouldn't have believed was within my reach.

When the lights dimmed and the crowd roared, I was transported into a world where nothing felt beyond my reach. I might not have been the stereotypical macho man at school, and I was still discovering myself socially. But here, on the rink, I knew—I just knew—that I could shine and be whoever I wanted to be. I had to give it my all. There was no room now for fault or failure, doubt or hindsight; there was only this moment—my chance to prove to everyone what I was capable of. Every muscle in my body propelled me forward. The blend of pleasure and pain, agony and ecstasy, surged through my senses with every graceful turn. After I landed my first double jump in a competition, and boy, was this the time to do it, I saw Lynda in the corner of the rink, jumping and screaming for me. After that, I gave my performance everything I had. But was it enough?

Before the competition, none of the other skaters had considered me, an unknown, to be a threat. It was more like, "Jayson, who?" So, when the scores started coming through, indicating I would win, I couldn't believe it. At my first significant competition, I had caused a major upset. Not only was the defending champion knocked into second position, but Grant Lawrence, the state champion of Victoria and the National Primary champion from the previous year, failed even to make the podium! I felt for him but was happy to be on the podium with my teammate, Mark Kinzett, who had beaten me in the state qualifier but missed the medal presentation.

My parents cheered, yelling my name at the top of their lungs. I could hear them, yet it seemed distant, as if from another world. My coach, Lynda, was tearful and joyful, jumping and embracing me. The tingling excitement that coursed through me was a welcome jolt amid the electrifying atmosphere where I now stood center stage. Skaters, whom I had only dreamed of talking to during the week, approached me to congratulate me on my performance. They were like gods to me, figures I had heard about from afar who commanded immense respect in the sport.

Mark Lind, a friend of Lynda's and one of the top coaches in our country at the time, draped an arm around me and said, "Aren't you clever." He was somewhat of a mystery to me, knowing he coached some skaters I admired. But there was something about him that eluded my grasp. Was it the scent of cigarettes mingled with cologne or how he regarded me? I couldn't pinpoint it, but I sensed this wouldn't be the last I'd encounter him. Ron Irving, coach and father of Paul Irving, standing with Lynda, also eagerly gave me a pat on the back, a highlight of the moment. At that age, I only knew

Paul Irving as the best skater in the country. Little did I know within three years, he would be my fiercest competitor.

> I stood in the marshaling area at Jayson's national competition with another Australian coach, Ron Irving. Jay had just completed his routine exceptionally well. I vividly remember the look on Ron's face as he exclaimed, 'My god, Sparky' (his nickname for me, given my last name was Flint), 'Where on earth did he come from?' He was completely blown away... LYNDA FLINT

1982 Nationals - Carol Jessop, Neale Warr & Jayson

I seemed lost in a dream's hazy fog for the remainder of the year. Upon returning to school, I was interviewed by the local newspaper, the Journal, marking my first appearance in black and white print. The picture was a comedy of errors: my hair was a disaster, looking like I had just rolled out of bed and forgotten what a brush was—ironic, considering I used to carry one in my schoolbag! And my face! Despite my slim build, it appeared strangely swollen, as if I were holding my breath with cheeks ready to burst. It was not exactly the glamorous debut I had hoped for, but it did provide some laughs at school. In recognition of my dedication and the nice trophy I brought home from nationals, my father promised me the Snyder skates I had long dreamed of. I would finally be among the 'elite' with these 'super skates' on every skater's wish list. It was all a bit overwhelming, but my coach, never one to rest on her laurels, intensified our training for the next six months, setting even loftier goals for the future, and I was up for it.

Lynda predicted my international debut within three years, showcasing her foresight that consistently amazed me. Over the following years, she challenged me artistically and technically, urging me to explore innovative techniques and styles of music to perform. She was deeply immersed in the music scene, often playing me a record and suggesting how perfect it would be for skating. My eyes would widen in wonder at her ideas. In 1982, when I won my first nationals, I skated to Elton John's 'Funeral for a Friend.' I vividly remember hearing the music for the first time in our living room at home. My mom stood beside me with a frown; she wasn't fond of it, and I was uncertain. It felt somewhat sad initially, but as we listened, its intensity grew, sending chills down my spine.

I realized she had chosen the perfect music for me, and from that moment, I trusted her instincts completely.

> *Unbelievably, when Jayson first started learning, he showed no interest in artistic expression. All he wanted to do was jump and spin. I would hold his arms above his head, trying to help him improve his artistic form, but as soon as I let go, his arms would flop down to his sides and flap around like chicken wings. Determined, I would grab them again and stretch them back above his head.*
>
> *One day, as I held his arms up, I thought, "Jayson, don't you dare drop them again." He looked at me with a mischievous glint in his eye, and I looked right back, daring him to keep them up. As soon as I let go, he started to drop them again, but instead of frustration, we both burst out laughing...*
> LYNDA FLINT

Our successes continued and peaked with another National title win in the Advanced Men's category at the 'Glass House' in Melbourne in 1984 (also known as the Melbourne Entertainment Center). However, I had missed out on the '83 title, partly due to letting early success get to my head. I was determined not to repeat that mistake. Competing in the junior category in my second year exposed me to pressure I wasn't unprepared for. I vividly recall standing in the stadium at the Parks Recreation Center in South Australia, with crowds cheering and my legs trembling uncontrollably as I awaited my music to begin, forcing myself to pat them down for composure. Despite entering the event undefeated all year with new tricks and overwhelming support, my nerves got the better of me. Boy, did I skate like shit! I was also competing against my neighbor, John. The pressure was certainly on there, as our friendship had strained, and we were skating at different clubs under different coaches. I skated first in the event, and my scores were, well, let's say… not significant compared to what I had received all year. John skated second, and he skated very well. There were squeals of joy when his scores were revealed; many knew he'd beaten me, and deservedly so.

In retrospect, missing out on the '83 title turned out to be the best thing for my career at that time. It grounded me, built my character, and made me appreciate the wisdom in my father's words: "No matter the outcome, keep pushing yourself and never take success for granted." This advice has kept me grounded ever since.

Although the performance in Adelaide was frustrating, the year was both challenging and rewarding. Just weeks before traveling interstate, I received the prestigious 'Outstanding Achievement Award' from Roller Sports Victoria, recognizing my accomplishments in my first year in the sport. To my knowledge, no other skater had received this award in their first year, and I was blown away to receive it. It wasn't just a little trophy but a huge two-tiered one, the biggest I'd ever seen. Yet, more significant moments of joy and hardship were still to come.

Junior Boys - Jayson, Neale & John

In January 1984, I had the privilege of meeting one of the greatest athletes in our sport, Scott Cohen, from the USA. He had just achieved a No. 2 ranking at the World Championships in Texas. As a teenager, I had repeatedly watched a video of the event and was in awe of the performances.

Both Tim McGuire and Scott became my immediate favorites for different reasons: Tim for his powerful aggression, speed, and technical perfection, and Scott for his artistic excellence, delivering performances that were both powerful and emotional. Scott became the inspiration behind my creative freedom and the most successful male artistic skater in history, winning five individual world titles. His style was reminiscent of the ballet stars who had left a lasting impression on me as a youngster.

> *For me, it was primarily about the music—interpreting it and elevating it to a new level. Obviously, the jumps and spins were crucial for scoring, but I wanted to elevate my performance by incorporating artistry and unique expressions of myself through the music.*
>
> *I think my inspiration was deeply internal, something that came from within, as if I was born to do it. I just loved skating so much. I wasn't THE BEST jumper, and I wasn't THE BEST spinner but I was strong in all three. The balance was really important, and that was my strength.*
>
> *I was happiest when I performed it in front of thousands of people with no restrictions, boundaries, or worries... SCOTT COHEN.*

Scott was in Australia with his coach, Jerry Walters. Both were pale after a cold US winter and thoroughly enjoying the Australian summer. A clinic was being held in Adelaide at the Skateline Modbury rink during the competition I was to contest, aptly named M.I.A.M.I (Modbury Interstate Artistic Meet Invitational). Despite having a broken arm from a training session accident, I participated in the camp, determined to seek Scott's and Jerry's undivided attention at every moment.

He performed several exhibitions throughout the camp, leaving everyone in awe, including our top skaters. One of his routines was to Elaine Paige's version of "Send in The Clowns." Everything about that performance was breathtaking. It was the first time I remember watching someone skate and feeling my jaw drop in amazement. Scott had an undeniable charisma, attracting admiration from everyone, and I couldn't help but admire him for that, too. This was the first time I had experienced anything on skates as intimate and alluring as Scott's performances, and the impact on my thinking moving forward was life-changing.

M.I.A.M.I. was my first competition since the previous championships in Adelaide, marking a fresh return. With a new program and beginning to shed my boyish looks, Lynda choreographed a routine for me to "Toccata" by Sky. I begged her for this music because it was frequently played on the TV before I went to school. Whenever I saw it, I would jump and dance around the living room, much to my younger brother's amusement, who called me an 'idiot' for it! In my opening sequence of that routine, I would bend my knees and lean forward, mimicking playing a piano with big, dramatic arm movements. It felt strange at first, but Lynda was right—the crowd cheered every time!

My jumping wasn't confined to our living room. When shopping with Mom, I would start performing skating maneuvers if she left me standing still for more than a moment. Mom would shudder and tell me to "cut it out immediately." Typically, with a sharp tug on my arm, she looked around to ensure nobody was looking. I know she must have been embarrassed, having a teenage boy jumping around in public for no reason. That was just me; I couldn't help it. I loved to jump on my feet, always attempting more challenging elements that I couldn't do on skates, leading to frequent falls and crashes into store shelves.

> We'd be going through the shopping center and Jayson would be in front and he'd be doing spins and jumping up and down on his feet, pretending to be doing axel's or whatever and people were looking and I'd be saying, 'Please Jayson, don't embarrass me.' But every time we went shopping the same thing happened so, he was just skate mad. I couldn't do much about it... Mom

Anyway, back to M.I.A.M.I. A highlight for many of us was the private lessons with Jerry, where Scott trained. I had never seen a true international skater perform, executing a triple jump to perfection or spinning with such speed and fluidity. Other top skaters from interstate, notably Linda A'Court, also shared this time. Melanie, Lynda, and I often sat on the sidelines, marveling at their skills and using them as a gauge to base our preparation for the years ahead. Melanie was already one of the few girls executing the double loop jump and performing it in combination, cementing her status as a rising star.

Sharing the floor with Scott at that age was a significant turning point for me, playing a vital role in shaping the direction I wanted to take. From then on, I knew I wanted to compete at a world meet. There was no hesitation in my mind —competing at worlds, being part of the Australian team, and winning a medal became my newest fixation and goal. Exposure like this is crucial for young athletes, especially in Australia, where international headliners are rare. The words written on my participation certificate by Scott and Jerry also left a lasting impact. I pinned it to my bedroom wall and read it daily as an affirmation, inspired by their hint that they would 'see me at Worlds in the future.'

> *"My highlight was the skate camps in Adelaide and Frankston; they were always so much fun. We'd catch the bus to South Australia and get billeted out with families at different homes each year because we couldn't afford to fly, with all the other skating expenses adding up. Mom was already working three jobs! But M.I.A.M.I was the ultimate camp, skating alongside Scott Cohen…"*
> *JENNY DOWNARD (COXHILL)*

Immediately after the meet in Adelaide, we headed home to attend another skating camp with over a hundred skaters from around Australia. It was the Christmas school holidays, and we were the busiest we'd ever been during the break. Shane loved all the traveling around, as we got to do some sightseeing and other fun stuff. It certainly beats riding our bikes down at the park daily.

However, an interstate coach, Mark Lind, one of the featured coaches at the camp, was about to impact my life profoundly. Mark was training most of the elite skaters in Australia, and speculation was that he would move to Melbourne to become a full-time coach at our club, Roller City. During the summer camp, he got to know my family well, and I couldn't wait for confirmation of his move. I was a massive fan of his top skater, Linda A'Court, who had already represented Australia at three world championships, becoming the first Australian female athlete to make the top ten in the world and achieving this milestone at fourteen. She was one of the most stunning women I had ever seen — my new teenage crush began! This admiration made things difficult, as Linda was Jenny's rival, and I adored them both!

The rumored move of Mark Lind to Melbourne proved true. This meant that Linda and another of his loyal skaters, Christine Hales (my soon-to-be girlfriend for a brief time), would also move with him. When I realized I could train with them daily, I felt life couldn't get much better.

'Jayson was ALWAYS getting the attention, the little brat!'

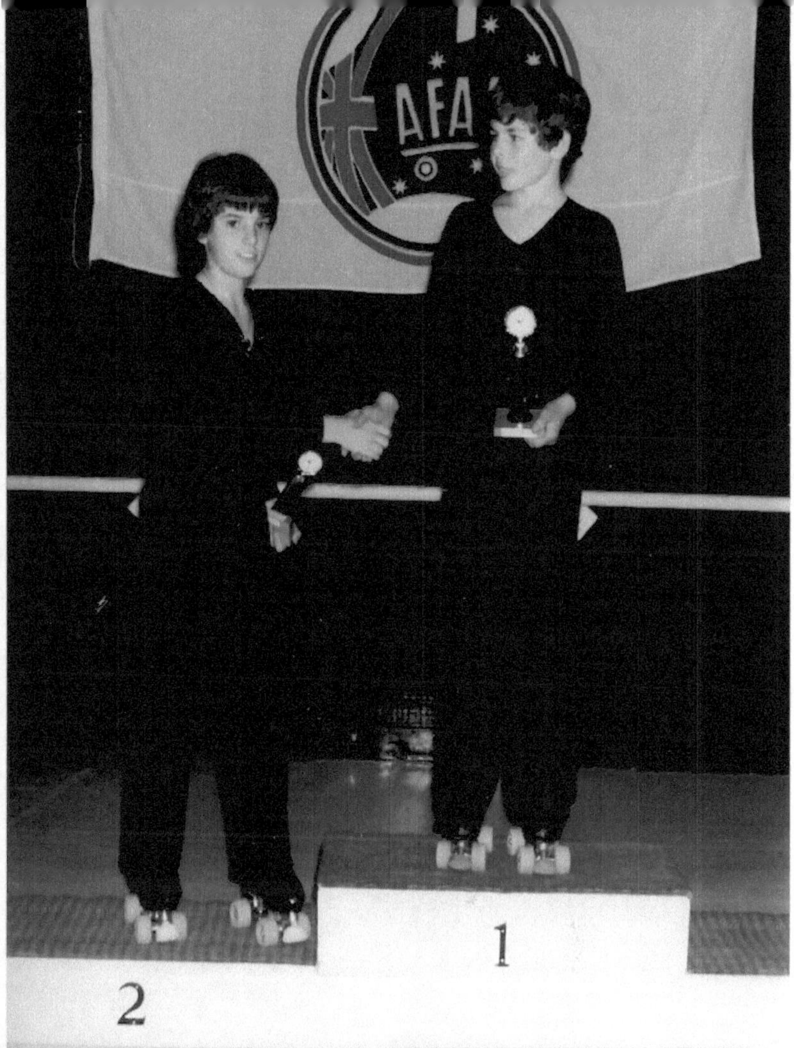
AFA
1
2

Have a Coke and a smile.
Coca-Cola
2HD
VICTORIAN CHAPTER
VICTORIA

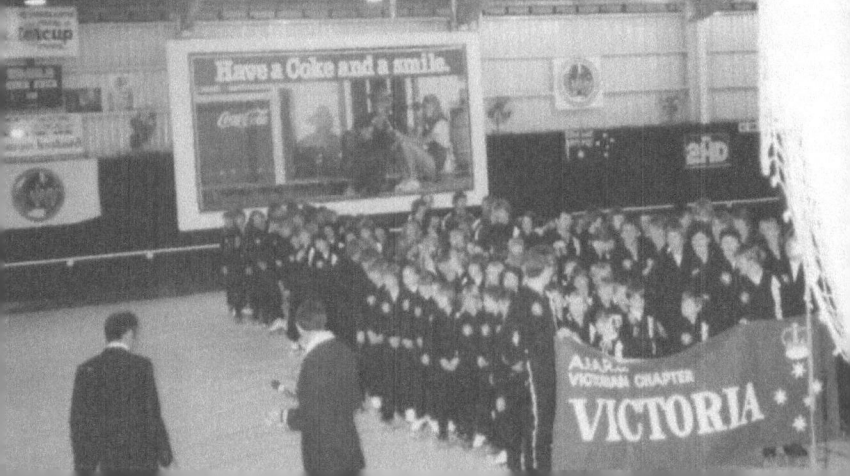

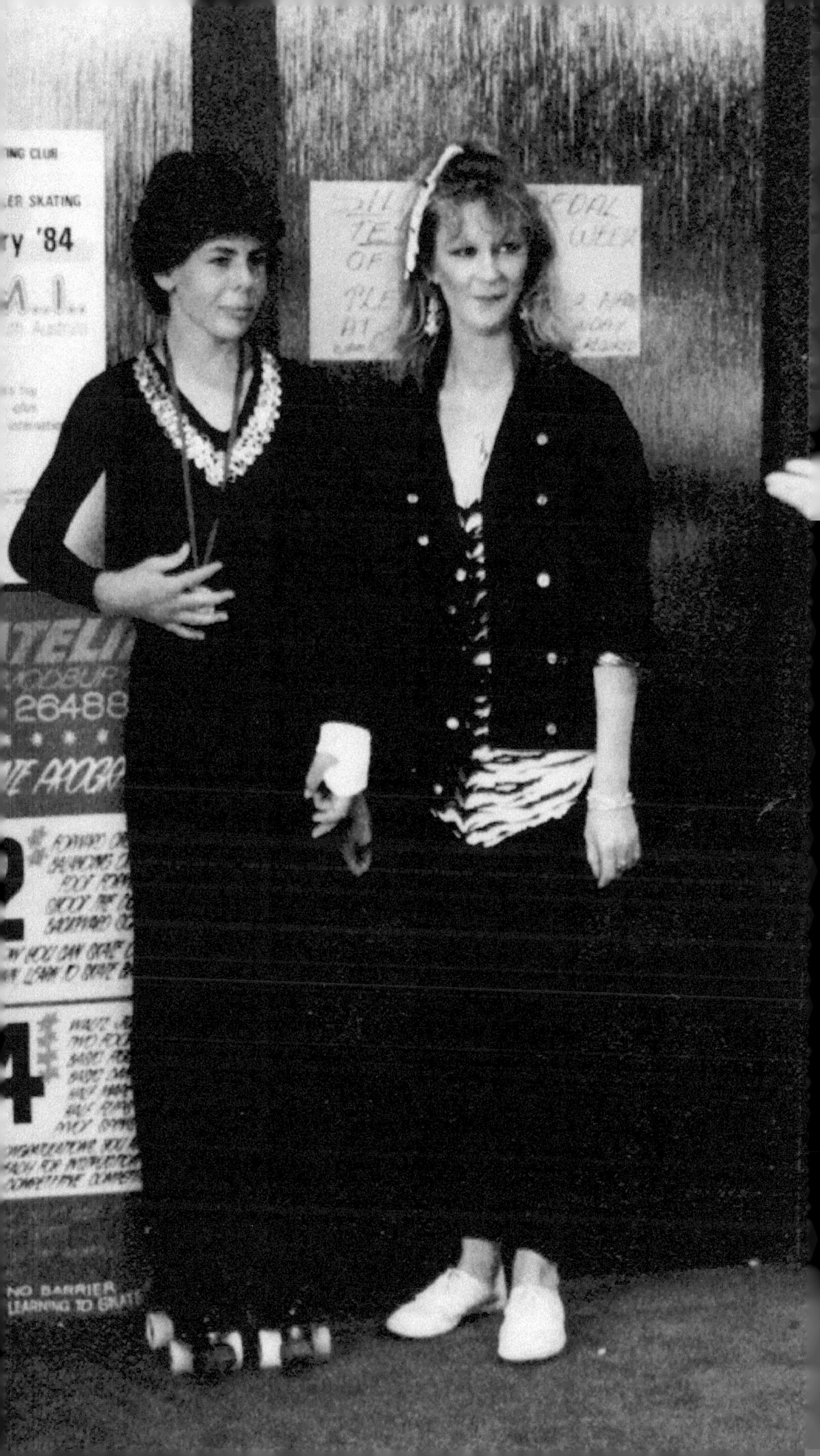
ING CLUB
ER SKATING
ry '84
26488
NO BARRIER
LEARNING TO SKATE

3

SECRET LIFE ON THE INSIDE

With Lind's arrival in Melbourne, word quickly spread throughout the skating community that he would coach me. It was a reasonable assumption, but nothing could have been further from my intentions. I vowed never to leave Lynda, wanting to make my international debut with her by my side. The thought of ending our relationship was heartbreaking. She was my coach, my creator, and my mentor. The idea of leaving her felt insulting and a betrayal. But my parents saw things differently. They believed switching coaches was in my best interest, as Mark could propel me to new heights.

There is no doubt in my mind that Mark himself had a heavy hand in this decision. He played a very influential role in the sport, adding weight to the decision. He was also living at our house, and nightly, there would be discussions about my skating at the dinner table and what he could do for me. Reluctantly, I bowed to the pressure, even though the idea of separating from Lynda was more painful than I could bear. Too cowardly and upset to tell her, my parents broke the news. One afternoon before training, I sat with my parents in the rink, awaiting Lynda's arrival. When she came, they went into the office to have a painful conversation with Lynda about me leaving her. She hurriedly left the rink in tears, and my heart broke for her. Dad reappeared shortly after; his eyes filled with emptiness.

> *When Jayson's parents approached me about them sending him to be coached by Mark, I completely lost the plot. I think I cried for a week straight. I felt so sorry for Bev and Col; I never meant to put them in that position, but I couldn't help it. I was actually in favor of Jayson moving on to improve his skating. I had been considering reaching out to Scott Cohen's coach in America and pleading for him to take Jayson under his wing — though I knew it was a bit fanciful.*
>
> *My reluctance stemmed from not wanting Jayson to train with Mark; I simply didn't trust the man. Unfortunately, there was nothing I could do about it... LYNDA FLINT*

Fate was stirring events in my life once again, as the introduction of Mark Lind was about to change my life in more ways than any of us could have imagined.

There was no question: Mark Lind knew the international circuit I craved. I didn't take long to become engrossed in his collection of skating videos from various world championships. Once he settled into his own home, I would borrow his videos and study them daily, determined to learn every skater's program by heart. In part, I was drowning my sorrows over losing Lynda by diving headfirst into the excitement of Mark's experience. However, I quickly built a solid student-coach relationship with him and began to thrive, just as he'd suggested to my parents I would.

I learned more about the great Tim McGuire by watching Mark's videos. I started to model my jumping technique on his to emulate his perfect triple jumps, but I was only doing doubles. Tim was the World Champion consecutively from 1981 to 1983. I remember telling Mark how I would love to be able to execute triple jumps like Tim and how great it would be to meet him one day. To my surprise, Mark had Tim's address. I was writing a letter to my new hero within minutes of mentioning it. That was one of the bonuses of being taught by Mark; he seemed able to grant my every wish. Whether Mark could take me to the heights of McGuire remained to be seen, but it was all part of the journey I had, in part, chosen to take and was destined to follow.

To my delight and surprise, I received a reply from Tim in Rochester, Michigan, within weeks. It was incredible; I was not yet fourteen years old—just a kid from a Melbourne suburb—and suddenly, I received mail from a world champion. The moment I saw the envelope addressed to me with a US postage stamp and Tim's name in the left-hand corner,

I froze for a moment, then jumped for joy and ran straight to my room to read it. Sitting on the side of my bed, I stared at the envelope for what seemed like an eternity before finally opening it. I must have read the letter at least a dozen times. It was inspirational, filled with the words of wisdom I needed to hear. Tim reminded me to "work on your spins" and expressed his excitement that I was "striving for excellence." More than that, the letter was personal—sincere and genuine, as if we had been friends for years. I still have it, even though I never actually met Tim. Mark seemed capable of opening so many doors for me, significantly contributing to the direction of my life.

By September of that year, my sister and her fiancé, Dave, announced they would marry earlier than expected, causing much panic for my mother. Naturally, she wanted the day to be Leanne's most beautiful and perfect memory. And it was. On September 29, my sister, looking like a fairy tale princess, married in a ceremony that brought tears to many eyes. For Mom, this was particularly special because it didn't (and doesn't) seem like any of her other children would marry anytime soon.

Mom fussed, pampered, and organized the four brothers to scrub up to our shining best, even if I had chosen something a little unconventional to wear. I desperately wanted to be dressed in something different. Looking back at the photographs, there's no question that I succeeded. I wore a gray sweater with an off-pink, gray-striped shirt and a gray leather tie to finish the look. That was okay, but I don't know what I thought when I chose my pants. They were a shade of pink—yes, pink! Go the '80s! Initially, I wanted to wear lemon, but my older brother Tony was wearing lemon, which gave off heavy Miami Vice vibes before it was even a thing, so to keep in the pastel shades, I selected pink. I can only say they were one of my many fashion faux pas of the glam '80s.

I had the job of capturing Leanne's special day on video. Equipped with our newly purchased shoulder-held handy cam, I navigated through the crowd like a pro, poking the camera into many unwilling faces. Another perk of skating was learning how to use the camera. Dad filmed almost everything at every competition; when he couldn't, it was up to me. I had a side hustle of copying footage onto VHS and BETA videotapes for skaters and families, selling them for a few dollars to save money for skating trips.

ROLABOI, REVIVAL

After the reception, we returned to our home with the rest of the wedding party for a few drinks to wrap up the night. It didn't take long for things to get rowdy at the party, and I could see there would be a lot of cleaning up to do. Since I had to train early the next day, a drunken Mark suggested I stay overnight and go to training directly in the morning. I begged Mom to let me stay, but she was reluctant. However, since it wasn't unusual for me to stay at Mark's house, she eventually threw her hands in the air and said,

"Fine. Go pack a bag and your training clothes, and don't mess around."

I was thrilled I could go and spent most of the late hours lazily watching skating videos before drifting off to sleep. Meanwhile, Mark continued drinking wine with his friend Sharon at the kitchen table across from where I was lying on the couch. It had been quite a day.

Many have questioned, and many will continue to wonder, why I've chosen to write about the following incident. After twenty years of avoiding these painful memories, writing has become my way of confronting and releasing this issue, hoping to find some closure. What happened can never be undone, and I deeply regret not confiding in my parents then. It felt like too much was at stake, and I wanted to hold on to whatever little I had. I didn't have the strength to tell them back then, but I feel ready and courageous enough to put it down on paper. I hope that it will encourage other victims of abuse to come forward and seek help and advice, share their pain with someone who can help, help them move on with their lives, and perhaps even put an end to such events.

Anyway... long before I had the chance to experience the beauty of intimacy, someone influential in my life took that away from me in exchange for a fleeting moment of self-indulgence. You might say, "It happens all the time," and dismiss it, but have you ever considered what it's like to be the victim? When it happens, the impact is enduring—a painful memory that haunts you. I was fourteen, and I was a victim in a helpless situation with no answers in sight. When and where the incident occurred are unimportant details, but it's not hard to connect the dots. Unfortunately, due to defamation laws in Australia, I can't disclose who the perpetrator was. However, what happened—did happen, and I bear the scars to prove it.

I awoke suddenly one evening, away from the confines of my own home, aware of a figure lying very close to me, holding my hand. I wasn't sure what to think, so I just tried to go back to sleep. But sleep was not to be. The person had started to kiss me, touch me, massage me, and thrust against me. I wasn't sure if alcohol played a significant role in this situation, but I was equally sure that it was no excuse for what was happening. Naturally, I was terrified and started shaking helplessly. I couldn't grasp what he was doing. My initial fear was that if I resisted, there might be repercussions, or the person could become aggressive. I knew I couldn't match an adult's strength. The ordeal seemed to drag on endlessly. All I could do was pray for it to end. Unfortunately, I experienced sensations I had never felt before—a dreadful tingling throughout my body. I wanted to scream, to flee, to express the intense fear and anger coursing through me, but my fear paralyzed me, leaving me unable to defend myself.

Rape, abuse, and molestation were subjects I had little knowledge of and rarely even heard people talking about at the age of fourteen, let alone experiencing them myself. It was 1984, and discussions about such topics were still somewhat taboo, unlike today, where stories of abuse are frequently aired in the news. When my clothes were slowly being removed, I desperately wanted to render this person unconscious (and if I had the power, I indeed would have) and disappear from the world entirely—the initial terrifying seconds stretched into minutes that felt like hours. The vivid memories of their skin's smell and the taste of their breath that overwhelmed me continue to haunt me. I lacked the strength to push them away, and even if I had screamed, who would have heard? I was at least twenty minutes away from home by car, and it must have been three or four in the morning by then. It was when an attempt was made to penetrate me that I pulled myself away, burying my face in the pillow, crying until I had no energy left to sob. The selfish person lay beside me, moaning as they drifted asleep. At dawn, I stumbled to the bathroom, retching and trembling as I confronted my shattered reflection in the mirror, staring back at me with disbelief.

In the overwhelming dismay and confusion that ensued, I grappled with what this meant for my sexuality, my life, and my family—essentially, its implications for the world at large.

Was it acceptable? Who should I confide in? After I finished vomiting and dry heaving, I wrapped myself in a blanket and curled up on their living room couch.

Hours later, as it was time to head to the rink, there was a knock at the door. Linda A'Court stood there, staring at me with a concerned gaze. "Are you okay, Jay?" she asked. Moving closer, she gently touched my forehead. "You should call your dad and ask him to come and get you right away," I called my dad. When he asked if I was alright, I said, "I've been feeling sick, that's all." From that day forward, I never spoke another word about it to him or my mother.

In the days following the incident, it took a wise friend to sense something was wrong and inquire about my well-being. Until recently, Mary was the only person I had confided in about what happened, and she was deeply moved to tears upon hearing the details. I pleaded with her to keep it between us, and though she urged me to speak to my parents or the police, I couldn't bring myself to face the shame or hurt my parents.

Later, I suspected Mary had spoken to my dad when he eventually asked while driving to the rink one day if anyone had 'interfered' with me. I was mistaken. Mary had honored her promise; she hadn't said anything to him, and I had lied. I couldn't bring myself to confess the truth to my father then. Perhaps it's too late for any action, but I no longer want to remain silent or carry this burden alone. Life is too short. This person stole my innocence.

Some may think I was young and misunderstood what happened, but I was aware. I know it was wrong. An injustice occurred, and its impact remains with me, impossible to erase. Like many others, I have endured the pain and continue to carry it.

> We knew something was wrong but we just didn't know what. He was always moody and withdrawn, and we knew something was up, but we never imagined that something like that had happened to him. If we had known, we would have done something about it right away. But finding out twenty years later... well, I was under the doctor's care for months after I found out.
>
> I think you didn't tell us because you didn't want your skating career to be affected. You thought it might impact your skating, and that came first, regardless of what had happened. But I still believe you should have told us. We could have helped you through it, even over the years... *Mom.*

4

GROWING UP OVERNIGHT

After enduring the horrific abuse, I found myself struggling to cope with what had happened. My behavior at school and the rink suffered greatly. I had trouble concentrating in class under the watchful eyes of teachers and during skating sessions. Barely passing Year 9, my school reports consistently noted my lack of focus. It was clear that I faced a rocky year ahead. Despite my love for skating, I began to doubt whether I could continue, and the one thing that I cherished was in great jeopardy. The sport demanded immense physical and mental strength, and I wasn't sure if I had what it took to persevere.

However, within a year of starting to work with Lind and putting aside my mental health challenges, I began to focus on what I loved most: skating. Things started to fall into place. I earned the opportunity to participate in my first international meet by invitation, a significant milestone. Additionally, I had the honor of performing at the opening ceremony of the Australian Games, broadcast live on Channel 7 from the Entertainment Center in Melbourne. It marked my debut on live television, requiring extensive preparation. Alongside Linda A'Court, Simon Reeves, and Melanie Thomas, we represented Roller Sports, even though it wasn't a competitive sport in the Games. We performed before a daunting audience of eight thousand people, part of a larger group that included over two hundred dancers and athletes from various sports. The entire performance, meticulously orchestrated and choreographed, showcased our skills in a twenty-minute demonstration. Being in front of such a huge crowd was surreal, but we all basked in the limelight.

The selections for the World Team in 1985 took place in Brisbane, where a dedicated competition was held for skaters nominated as potential national team members. Mark entered me into the trials primarily to gain experience and prepare for the upcoming year. Little did he know my ambitions went far beyond gaining mere expertise.

But shortly before the trip, I was having an off day, and Mark wasn't tolerating it. He kept pushing me, but I had reached my limit. After falling several times while attempting a triple jump, he gave me a hard time near the barrier. My mom was only a few feet away, and the frown on her face said everything. Mark grabbed my leg, pushed me into an arabesque position, and started instructing me. His idea of instruction, however, involved pushing, prodding, and yelling in my ear. I had heard as much as I could, so I dropped my leg. He grabbed it and pulled it back into place, placing his hand higher up between my legs and squeezing me. I flinched and reacted by kicking him in the stomach and pushing him away. He was furious and groaned like a little girl. My mother, not knowing what had happened, was also furious. She leaned over the barrier, grabbed me by the t-shirt, pulled me over the wall, dragged me out of the rink, still in my skates, kicking and screaming like a baby, and threatened I would never skate again.

I did skate again and was only grounded from the rink for 24 hours. But it was a sign that with the good times, there would also be bad times and more of them. In hindsight, it was the perfect time for me to tell my parents what had happened, but I was only weeks away from my very first world trials. When I weighed up what mattered, skating always won, in fear of losing what I did love.

Accompanied by my mom, we flew up to Brisbane for the world trials. It was our first time flying, and it was a nerve-wracking experience for both of us. To my surprise, on the morning of my competition, my father and brother Shane showed up to support me unexpectedly. It was a touching gesture I hadn't anticipated, but it was typical of my father to surprise us thoughtfully.

I earned second place in the short program, performing to 'One Night in Bangkok,' just behind Paul Irving. It was surreal to compete against someone who, just two years prior, I admired as an idol. Securing this position ensured my place on the World Team, with David Morrison in third and Simon in fourth. Mark was devastated by the outcome. He had pinned high hopes on Simon going to Italy for figures and free skating, but sadly, it wasn't meant to be. Fortunately, it meant I was off to my first World Championship at just fifteen years old.

This unexpected achievement caused quite a stir, not only at the event but also back home. Relationships began to strain, and the competition among Mark's skaters intensified dramatically. In this individual sport, you need a "take no prisoners" attitude; otherwise, you risk falling off the wagon and being left behind.

Securing a spot on the Australian team meant another journey by plane, this time to Italy—a thrilling prospect as it marked my debut in international competition. But the question of funding loomed large. I knew this was a constant worry for my parents, as it was for many others, but we always managed to find ways to raise the necessary funds for these journeys. During this period, the strain on our family intensified as my siblings matured, became more independent, and pursued greater freedoms, becoming less involved in our family life. My mom became somewhat focused on my sport and my pursuit of dreams, possibly losing sight of these changes in our family dynamic.

Following this victory, the late Graeme Shepherd invited fellow skater Christine Hales and me to compete at the International Trophy Day competition. Being invited to Trophy Day was a fantastic opportunity, and it also served as a chance to test my wings on a trip to New Zealand before the longer journey to Italy. My parents allowed me to travel alone, with Mark as my chaperone. This experience marked my introduction to international competition and granted me my first taste of actual travel and independence. Being alone with Mark made me somewhat uneasy, but having Chrissy and Simon on the trip eased my nerves. However, one night at the bar, Mark placed his hand on my leg as I ordered a Coke. In a reflexive action, I threw my drink over him. The shock on his face terrified me, and I couldn't believe my reaction. I hurriedly ran to my room, jumped into bed, and hid under the blankets.

Artistic skating wasn't a high-profile sport in New Zealand, like in many other countries. However, the competition in Palmerston North was tough. My main competitor was Simon from my club, who seemed more determined than ever to prove he should have been on the world team instead of me. The result never sat well with Mark, who viewed my participation as secondary. In Palmerston, Simon skated exceptionally well, delivering the performance he had aimed for during the trials and clinching first place. I ended up second.

After the competition, Chrissy and I traveled by train to Auckland, where we were invited to perform at the exhibition show Skate in Manukau. Meanwhile, Mark and Simon flew there, which suited me just fine. During the Palmerston competition, I befriended Richard Legge, who was two years younger than me, thirteen. We became close friends, but unexpectedly, this friendship came with a price—I started facing remarks about my sexuality. It was bewildering and hurtful, especially since I didn't have a girlfriend and was socializing with someone my age. The taunts extended beyond the skating community to the schoolyard, where I had endured similar insults like 'sissy' and 'poofter' throughout my primary years.

Back home, I confided in my dad about the ridicule one night. His advice was straightforward yet reassuring.

> *Listen, Jay," he said calmly. "You know who you are and what you're not. You don't need to prove yourself to anyone else.*

It didn't solve the problem, but having his support meant everything to me. Dad didn't always need to say much; sometimes, just a look from him conveyed everything I needed to hear. But I think it was a little more challenging for Mom; I'm not sure she believed it or wanted to believe I could be gay.

> *People kept telling me that Jayson was 'different' but I don't know whether I wanted to believe it or not but I didn't. He is my son. Someone else said to me 'Your son's gay' and I said, 'No he's not. And, if that's the life he chooses, that's his business... Mom.*

Our departure for the World Championships came swiftly. I was boarding a jumbo jet headed for the other side of the world, and it also meant no school for three to four weeks. I was over the moon about that! Our training regimen intensified significantly in the weeks leading up to the event. While

I dedicated myself to rigorous practice at the rink, Mom indulged in a shopping spree, expanding her wardrobe tenfold. It was heartening to witness her excitement for the trip.

Few knew of the personal battles she had fought in her life. Before my skating journey, she had endured periods of hospitalization, battling depression following the loss of a young child and her former husband. Her upbringing was equally challenging, marked by uncertainty as she navigated foster homes from a young age and began working at a hospital when she was only thirteen. Roller skating didn't just serve as a distraction for her; some might even say it became an addiction that "saved her life."

Surprisingly, one of the most challenging items to secure was a pair of navy-colored dress shoes required for our official Australian team suits. Our ensemble included full pants, a jacket, and a choice of tie or cravat for arrival and departure. The suit jacket was a vivid garden green, paired with a golden yellow shirt and white collar. I opted for a blue leather tie, silently expressing my disapproval of the other colors in our attire.

Finding those elusive blue shoes took us to the city by train, where we finally found a suitable pair. Exhausted from our search, I fell asleep on the train ride back, only waking moments before our stop. Rushing off, I began the walk home with Mom, who suddenly stopped in her tracks. "Did you forget something?" she asked rhetorically.

A lump formed in my throat as my stomach sank. "Shit. My bags," I yelled. Indeed, after all that effort, I had left my shoes and many other purchases on the train. We tried the "lost and found," hoping for a stroke of human kindness. Our efforts were in vain. Ultimately, I had to settle for a pair of black shoes we spray-painted in navy. It wasn't ideal, but it was better than nothing, and I knew better than to complain.

Getting the funds together for travel was a challenge, but we managed with help from our friends. Local skating clubs organized fundraising events, the most successful of which were spit roast barbecues at our house. Donated food and drinks drew around one hundred fifty attendees, each contributing ten dollars or more. The events were a hit socially, especially with my brothers, who appreciated the single-skater girls who attended.

Accompanied by Mom, Mark, and fellow skaters Simon and Chrissy, we set off for Italy. While not taught by Mark, Jenny Downard made the team in the ladies free skating, making our group from Victoria complete. While Simon had experience from two previous world meets, Chrissy and I were embarking on this journey for the first time, filled with excitement at every step.

Our journey included stops in Saudi Arabia, where armed guards boarded our plane, and a chaotic layover at Heathrow, where we missed our connecting flights due to bad weather. The planned helicopter transfer was canceled, forcing us onto a long bus ride across Heathrow to catch another flight to Italy.

Finally, upon boarding the last leg of our journey, we reunited with the rest of the Australian team. Racing to the gate due to our delayed connection, I glanced back to see my overwhelmed mom, tears in her eyes, struggling to keep up with her load. It was a poignant moment, made worse when we learned our flight was delayed after all the effort to catch it on time.

During all the chaos, I made a memorable mistake—I mistakenly grabbed another passenger's suitcase at the airport, thinking it was mine. Upon opening it, I was shocked to find it filled with lingerie and women's clothing! Tears welled up as I imagined my costumes lost. I briefly entertained the idea that my teammates were playing a prank on me, but reality set in when I learned my case was returning to Australia. It took days for it to return, but fortunately, we'd arrive days before the competition started, and I managed to retrieve it before our official preparations began.

Arriving in Rimini, the stunning Italian coastal resort with expansive beaches, was a delight. Our hotel was just steps from the beachfront, with a gelato store at the lobby's doorstep. And yes, it became a daily ritual to indulge in one. Once we shed our formal suits, we eagerly explored the local sights, making the most of our time before training officially began.

The local outdoor Skate Park, with its backdrop of the sparkling Mediterranean, hosted our first informal practice session. The salty breeze teased our skin, tempting us to head straight for the beach. It was during this session that the American team arrived. Though I hadn't met most of them, names like Tina Kneisley, Rick Monturo, Tammy Jerue, and Scott Cohen rang familiar. Excitement surged as I anticipated skating hard and making an impression on these seasoned competitors.

Scott was the first to approach Mark and comment on my inverted camel spin. I couldn't have been more grateful to Jenny for her help mastering that maneuver. Scott also remarked on how much progress I had made since his last visit to Australia two years ago, making the journey all the more worthwhile.

Italian skaters were relatively unknown in artistic roller skating at the time, except for figures like Michele Biserni, the World Champion in 1984 and a revered figure in Italy. The country was hungry for success, diligently nurturing skaters with immense potential. In 1985, Italy unveiled its dark horse, Chiara Sartori. At just fifteen years old, she exuded beauty, grace, and charisma, capturing the hearts of her nation and the world. Despite her petite frame, Chiara made a significant impact with her powerful performances.

Chiara's presence at the championships was transformative. She dominated the event and made history by winning three gold medals in her debut appearance across three events. She continued to reign as the top performer for the next three consecutive years, inspiring me deeply. Witnessing her achievements solidified my dream to become a World Champion and captivate audiences with my skating.

The event also marked a golden moment for Scott Cohen. After a setback in 1984 due to an ankle injury in the short program that kept him out of the rankings, Scott mesmerized the audience in Rimini, reclaiming the crown from his rival, Biserni. Scott was thrust into the spotlight with perfect scores of 6.0 and a display of sheer brilliance. Headlines hailed him as "Cohen, Poetry in Motion," sparking admiration and emulation among skaters worldwide, including myself. I was so eager to emulate my idols—Cohen, Biserni, and Sandro Guerra—in their skating techniques, hairstyles, and unique form.

My debut performance was a milestone not to be dismissed. I finished the competition with a ninth-place ranking in the senior division, competing against a formidable field of forty-one skaters as a fifteen-year-old kid. It validated the hard work and sacrifices my parents had made. Placing within the top ten filled me with determination to aim higher. I set my sights on breaking into the top five within three years—a lofty goal, perhaps, but one I was determined to achieve before my time 'ran out.' Little did I know this journey would span eighteen years on wheels, shaping my life profoundly.

> *I remember the comments from the judges in Rimini, especially from the overseas judges, particularly the Americans. They were impressed that Jayson combined artistry with the physical capability to perform the elements he attempted as a fifteen-year-old competing among the senior men. They remarked, 'It won't be long before this kid'll be up there with the rest. He'll very likely beat the rest.' And it turns out that they were right...*
> *JEFF JESSOP (Judge).*

ROLABOI, REVIVAL

In Rimini, I matured overnight, the haunting events of just a year ago feeling like a distant memory. As one of the youngest male athletes in the competition, surrounded by young adult skaters aged 17-28, the post-competition scene was all about parties, drinking, and, let's face it, sex! Well, and for some, during the competition, too! Being in one of Italy's famed beach resorts amplified the allure, with the town throbbing with energy that drew young souls into its nightlife hub.

At fifteen, I longed to plunge into the excitement, but navigating this world wasn't straightforward, with our mothers keeping watch like hawks. Alongside Chrissy, Madonna Armstrong, Jodie Johnson, Maria Giuffre, and Darren Ransom, we zipped through the streets on mopeds, weaving through traffic and evading our parents' eyes at all costs. None of us had driven a car or ridden a motorbike before, so this was a thrilling new challenge. Yet, it didn't reasonably compensate for missing out on the wild nights, so we had to have a few of our own.

> *While we were in Italy, I celebrated my 16th birthday, and Jayson played a crucial role in organizing a surprise party for me. It was such innocent fun, decorating the hotel room with toilet paper. There was lots of laughter and silliness, a testament to how much fun can be had with friends who, like Jayson, are still part of my life today...*
> JODIE JOHNSON (GARUFO)

At the same time, I was delving into another facet of life that was darker and more mysterious, akin to an unturned stone in my path. I soon realized that homosexuality was not uncommon within my sport. It would be wrong to suggest that all skaters were gay—such a blanket statement would be absurd—but it did exist, as in many other aspects of life. It was not something I had encountered openly and confidently before.

Despite its elegant appearance, skating demands incredible athleticism. I often pondered how top "straight" football or soccer players would fare in our arena, where endurance, strength, and grace must seamlessly blend. Perhaps in more artistic sports, there's a higher proportion of gay athletes compared to traditional "macho" sports. Still, I can assure you that there's a significant number of male skaters who are not gay at all—they participate purely out of love for the sport.

This lifestyle didn't intimidate me; I was primarily curious, especially given that alternative lifestyles were still stigmatized in Australia at that time. I always felt different from other boys my age from a young age. It seemed others sensed this, too, leading to gossip and taunts often. But in this environment, surrounded by others who likely faced similar challenges, I felt a sense of acceptance and an understanding of what I might be. I wasn't ready to openly discuss my identity, nor was I fully aware of my true sexuality, but among my male counterparts, my curiosity was hard to contain.

I had formed a close bond with one of my fellow skaters in Italy. My mother was pleasantly surprised and pleased to see us getting along well. Together, we indulged in everything

Italy offered: shopping, jewelery, gelato, swimming at the beach, and amusing ourselves by confusing the non-English-speaking staff in the stores with our silly accents. From the start of the trip, there was a growing fascination with someone of the same sex, a feeling that had not brought any understanding to the unjust event that had occurred less than a year before. I had never asked for it to happen, nor had I wanted it. But as my first European trip progressed, these new feelings began to surface, leading to a journey of self-exploration. Each day, I found myself more attracted to my friend. The unexplained urges and feelings I had experienced as a child became more apparent, and I gradually realized that he was becoming much more than just a friend.

My conflicting thoughts and emotions gradually crystallized into a profound realization. I no longer felt the need to hide behind walls. I had found someone to confide in and explore with. From that first touch, when our legs brushed against each other as we sat in the stands watching the competition, to the moped ride where my arms wrapped around him, even if only briefly, every moment sent tingles through me.

I knew this discovery wouldn't be readily accepted, but by the end of the championships, I had learned more about myself than I had ever imagined. I felt alive, not because of the physical aspect, but because I had unearthed the real me. I harbored no shame or regrets about my experiences. One of my biggest concerns was explaining this to my 'on and off again' girlfriend back home, Karen James. I was clueless.

Sadly, as the championships concluded, so did the relationship I had been navigating. I desperately wanted this newfound connection to last forever, but our team would part ways within days. We wouldn't see each other again for nearly a year, but we became good friends. I had fallen hard for someone, a feeling I had only flirted with back home, but this was different—real, consuming, and it left me feeling vulnerable. You might wonder about the skating. Well, let me tell you, it was no distraction; it amplified my entire experience in Italy. I felt like I was on top of the world, both on and off the rink.

Upon returning home, everything felt different. As I pushed my trolley through customs, gazing at the floor, I realized how much I had transformed. Beyond my experiences with my new friend, I no longer felt like a scruffy teenager; instead, I felt refined, with a newfound sense of purpose inspired by my time abroad. I began wearing a chain around my neck and a gold ring we had purchased together during our shopping stints in Rimini, symbols of a personal metamorphosis that caught my father's attention when he first set eyes on me. While he seemed preoccupied with our return, I sensed his awareness of these changes.

School became a different environment altogether. I felt disconnected from the usual norms without proclaiming anything at an assembly. Unsure of my identity, I noticed a shift in how I perceived things, perhaps because I was evolving while my surroundings remained static. Most noticeably, my relationships with my siblings at home seemed altered, never entirely returning to how they were, except Colin, who always nurtured me, encouraged me, and made me proud of who I was. While they sensed something different about me, I felt isolated, unable to confide in anyone except Mary. Fear of rejection kept me from openly discussing my sexuality with friends, adding to my loneliness. Suddenly, I felt like I was right back where I had been just a few months earlier—a deep hole with no way out.

School and skating became a disastrous mix the following year, in 1986. I'll admit, I skipped so many classes that the school was probably more surprised when I did show up! My parents kept pushing me to excel academically and in skating, but I couldn't muster any enthusiasm for schoolwork. While many successful athletes managed to juggle university degrees and high-level sports, that path just wasn't for me, and things didn't look like they were getting any better.

In 1985, I failed my year level and had to repeat it. My report card indicated I'd been absent for at least 90 days over the year. No wonder I failed! The second time around in Year 10, it was a struggle and embarrassing not to be entering Year 11 with the small group of friends I did have. I lost all interest in learning, and my attendance dropped drastically. By mid-term, I was quietly asked to leave the school. So, I did and found a part-time job at a sports store. Knowing I had disappointed my parents, who only wanted the best for me, was a blow to my pride. At first, it felt like a rush of freedom and a step forward, but reality soon set in. I longed for the camaraderie of school, especially those lunchtime moments on the oval with my friends. We'd blast '80s tunes on our beatbox, singing along to Cyndi Lauper songs and casually brushing each other's hair with my pink vent brush.

During this time, I faced growth-related challenges that caused numerous issues on the skating rink. My body was growing faster than my muscles could adapt, leading to several injuries over the year. One of these injuries forced me to withdraw from an event for the first time, which devastated me. Fortunately, I recovered quickly and was fit enough to compete by mid-year at the International Trophy Day during the next trip to New Zealand. However, injuries continued to plague me, including a torn hamstring and a pinched nerve in my shoulder. Dealing with these injuries was not the enjoyable side of the sport for me!

Trophy Day in Auckland marked a milestone for me as I executed my first perfectly clean triple jump—a triple toe loop (mape) and my first triple Lutz, although that was not perfectly clean. I had a false start during this competition. The triple-toe loop was my second element, and just as I was skating into the jump, the music suddenly stopped. Startled, I froze mid-jump and was called off the rink. I feared I had missed my chance to attempt the triple, but to my surprise, I was given another opportunity to give it a real shot.

I had been consistently landing it for about six weeks beforehand, so I was confident I could nail it despite falling on it the day before in the short program. The vivid memory of my first successful attempt remains clear as if it had happened just yesterday. It occurred during an afternoon training session at Roller City Frankston, where I relished the opportunity to 'show off,' especially when someone was watching. On this occasion, my audience was a fiery red-headed aunt of a good friend. With her eyes fixed on me, I lined up my second attempt and executed three rotations in the air with precision, landing gracefully on one foot, perfectly upright. The exhilaration of that moment was indescribable. It felt like the culmination of years of hard work, akin to the thrill of landing your first axel as a beginner. Exiting the jump, I couldn't contain my excitement—I screamed at the top of my lungs, clenched my fists, and fought back tears of joy.

Mastering this jump was crucial for me to elevate from a competent performer to a severe contender in the major leagues. At that time, only a few competitors in Australia, like Simon Reeves and Paul Irving, could consistently execute clean triple jumps. Knowing I needed to perform at least four triple jumps in competition to compete for medals internationally, my determination to conquer this challenge was relentless. When I started to falter on the triple jump, my mother, aware of my aspirations and challenges, even took me to a hypnotherapist. However, had she known about my previous struggles, she might have sought therapy earlier for something more significant.

Under the hypnotherapist's guidance, I engaged in a series of visual exercises aimed at entering a focused state, although I remained skeptical about achieving complete unconsciousness. Nevertheless, this experience reinforced my belief in the power of visualization. While visualization alone couldn't substitute for practice, repeatedly envisioning myself executing the perfect jump undoubtedly played a role in turning that vision into reality.

Unfortunately, my visualization didn't foresee that successfully executing the jump in competition would mark a significant turning point in my career. At the final stage of my performance in New Zealand, however, I suffered another, more severe hamstring tear. This injury sidelined me from skating for another three months, forcing me to withdraw from the '86 National Championships—a devastating blow. It also meant missing out on qualifying for the National Team's trip to Bogotá later that year. It was a bitter disappointment. I was an eager sixteen-year-old keen to showcase my new weapon, my triple jumps, to Paul Irving. No one outside our club in Australia had seen me do them so that it would have been unexpected. I was also eager to return to the Parks stadium in Adelaide, where I had performed poorly at my second nationals, and use my triple jumps to reclaim some closure on that chapter. But it wasn't meant to be. Such is the paradox of life—it seems unable to deliver success without dishing out the tough shit, too.

After Trophy Day, a party was thrown for the skaters and parents at a local nightspot owned by one of the officials. Initially a private affair, the venue opened to the public at 9 pm, which happened to be one of Auckland's most popular gay venues, 'Alfies.' Although the gay setting didn't bother me personally, it unexpectedly thrust me into an environment where my secret life felt exposed. Surrounded by images of naked men on the walls and the scrutinizing gazes of older men as the patrons mingled with the skating party, memories of past events I'd rather forget came flooding back.

I was torn; I didn't know whether to openly embrace my identity then and there or retreat into anonymity. I was surrounded by girls in our team and we were all dancing and having fun, but ultimately, I realized I wasn't ready to confront the complexities that being openly gay might bring to my life at that moment, even with my dad by my side.

'You know who you are and what you're not.'

5

MOVING ON

It took a long eight months for me to recover from my injuries fully. The agony of being unable to compete for a title at the National meet, especially after participating in my first World Championships, was overwhelming. It was even more complicated now that I had left school and dedicated myself to training. It felt like I was being punished for a crime I didn't commit. Despite this, I attended the national championships and competed in figures, but that was it. I was unable to detach myself from the event during my recovery completely, and Dad was still heavily involved in assisting and filming all the events. Ironically, I was awarded my first National 'Junior Male Athlete of the Year Award.' The trophy was presented to me by Roller Sports Australia President Con Galtos, a revered figure in Australian skating, at the Championships' opening. His encouraging words that "he expected to see a lot more of me in the future" lifted my spirits immensely, even adding,

> *No doubt you could become Australia's first World Champion.*

1986 Nationals Opening - Jayson & Con Galtos

This period marked the beginning of mounting tensions between my coach and others, stemming from unknown reasons, often because Mark had slagged off somebody or passed judgment. Notably, he was involved in a physical altercation with two other prominent male figures and a female at this championship. It became the talking point of the tournament, one that concerned many of the parents from our club. Consequently, we were asked to leave my beloved Roller City, and it was hard to say goodbye to all of our friends, but as this door closed, another opened.

My 'celebrity status' among my family skyrocketed when I was invited to be a guest judge on the popular kids' Saturday morning television show, The Early Bird Show. The show featured a roller skating segment, where kids competed each week for four weeks to win prizes. Alongside Kristie Backway and Warren Morrison, I was part of the judging panel, and we dressed up each week to appear on the show, feeling quite important.

We performed a demonstration at the beginning of the segment run, which was challenging in such a small space. It was our first experience performing live in front of cameras in an intimate setting alongside skating with Jenny Downard, which was a highlight for me. We performed 'Memory' from Cats, which ended very abruptly while I was skating, and the look on my face matched the blank stare I gave the cameras during the interview with a one-word answer. Fortunately, we left most of the talking to June Kinzett (Ison).

I was a massive fan of the TV show Prisoner (now known as Wentworth), which was filmed at the exact location of The Early Bird Show. I loved posing for photos outside the prison set and was thrilled to find a script lying on the ground one day, which I kept as a memento. I also claimed bragging rights over getting photos with the host, Daryl Cotton.

ROLABOI, REVIVAL

Early Bird Show 'Judges' - Warren, Kristie and Jayson

After being 'thrown out' of Roller City Frankston, we initially relocated to Skate World in Noble Park but had to move again within a year, and from that point on, the doors opening would no longer be there. I loved skating at Noble Park; it was close to home, and the floor was well-sized. We all settled in well and shared the floor with another leading coach and dear friend, Julie Brown. She also became very fond of Mark. However, things quickly turned sour, and our future at Skate World looked bleak. But I was determined to make the most of our time there. Just as I started hitting my stride again, I fell badly on my hand. Initially, I wasn't sure if it was broken, and my mom encouraged me to finish my lesson, which I did. However, the pain intensified, and I was taken to the hospital.

A few hours later, it was confirmed: I had broken my wrist and now had a fiberglass cast fitted.

This happened only a few weeks before the national championship in Perth, where I was set to compete against my main rivals, Paul Irving and Simon Reeves. It had been almost two years since our first lineup, and I wouldn't let a cast get in the way.

The cast on my arm didn't bother me at all. I had to adjust my costumes to accommodate it, but other than that, I was in top form. By the time the long program ended, the week was almost over, and I was sitting in second place behind Paul, with Simon close behind in third. Eight were in the Senior Men's division, and this was Simon's first competition since leaving Mark as his coach; he had returned to working with Charmaine, which only added to the pressure as Mark was determined I wouldn't be beaten this time in a turnaround of events.

I was skating to Vivaldi's 'Four Seasons,' a program I was very comfortable with. Opening with a solid double axel fired me up, and it was time to prove I could land the triple jumps and put pressure on Paul. I succeeded, but Paul's experience and stamina gave him the edge to maintain his top ranking. I never felt bad about losing to Paul; he was an Australian skating hero, 27 years old, while I was just 17, a new kid on the block, chipping away at what he had worked so hard to achieve.

After returning from Perth, things weren't going smoothly at Skateworld. Our group and coach had developed a reputation within the skating community that made us feel "unwelcome." It wasn't a great feeling; we just wanted to skate and do what we loved. In response, the parents of Mark's skaters formed a support group and collectively searched for a new training venue. With no rinks left for us to go to, many of us were left wondering where to go and what to do next.

As a last resort, we moved our newly formed club into a youth hall in Sandringham. It was an indoor netball court next to the athletics track and outdoor netball courts. The indoor court was so small that it took time to adjust. Soon, I felt it was impossible to attempt anything technically challenging, and I noticed a decline in my confidence and speed. Despite this, we made do. We named ourselves Skate Connection, and over the following year, we became a formidable team, winning almost every event we entered.

I decided to leave school midway through 1986 and worked at a sports store in the afternoons for about three months. The reality of leaving school hit hard; having a job meant I couldn't just head to the rink whenever I wanted, impacting my training hours. Things weren't ideal, but returning to school was out of the question. A vacancy came to my attention at a small clothing company looking for a junior assistant in the cutting room. The job piqued my interest since I had often fancied myself as a designer after finishing skating and the hours suited. Initially, it was a bit daunting, but my supervisor, Marlene Watson, was a free-spirited and open-minded individual who helped me ease into the position and embrace this new challenge.

My interest in fashion snowballed, and by 1988, I was astonished at the skills I'd developed through working at the factory. I spent most of my lunch hours in the sewing rooms, learning to use the industrial machines and construct garments. The ladies who worked there were genuinely kind and loved to help me as though I was their baby. There's no question that I was the youngest employee at EBCO Apparel. It was the best hands-on experience anyone could have asked for.

Before long, I made colorful and glamorous outfits for my boss's friends and Marlene. Often, I would be sent off during work hours to sew up something somebody wanted to wear out that weekend. I also started doing sample sewing for the company, which presented a fantastic opportunity to further my interests. In addition, our new club, Skate Connection, desperately needed a new club tracksuit. This allowed me to combine what I saw as my two main interests – skating and fashion – and I offered to make all eighteen tracksuits myself. I think I bit off more than I could chew by volunteering for this, but our garage at home was soon converted into a mini factory. I had two industrial machines on loan from work, a cutting table, and patterns everywhere. This also meant that the only time I had to work on the tracksuits was late at night, leading to several weeks of sleep deprivation. Despite the exhaustion, the tracksuits began to take shape just in time for our big reveal at the next state championship.

As we entered 1988, Roller Sports Australia was invited to perform a series of shows at the World Expo in Brisbane. Each of the three groups of fifteen skaters from Victoria, Queensland, and New South Wales was given a meager budget of $1,500 for costuming. Our group decided to pool our resources and create the most elaborate costumes we could imagine within our performance's "space theme" parameters. Mark developed a concept story for our thirty-minute show, centered around space travelers who land on a mysterious planet searching for a unique orb guarded by 'Baba Yaga' played by Tracey Perren from NSW.

Together with the parents of the skaters in the troupe, we worked tirelessly to create innovative garments that could rival the costumes in any Broadway show. The outfits were works of art, crowned with incredible headdresses and large flowing capes. They proved a huge success, attracting thousands of spectators daily at the Expo. The organizers were astonished at how we constructed such elaborate costumes, especially when the other groups of skaters presented themselves in traditional skating outfits.

In contrast, our multiple costume changes ranged from skin-tight suits to Lycra body sacks, hula-hoop dresses, Batman-inspired winged capes, and evil Star Wars-inspired alien creations, along with a fold-out spaceship my dad had created for us, four of the skaters emerged from it at the start of the show. All the effort was well worth it, firmly placing our group on the map in the skating fraternity and setting me on the right track toward my dream of becoming a designer.

JAYSON SUTCLIFFE

Rehearsal for 1988 World Expo - Felicity Martin & Jayson

My work in the clothing industry was progressing better than my skating career. The dramatic change in practice venues had taken its toll on many of us. The small size and poor floor surface created problems, even though the Skate Connection team had been successful locally. Following the 1987 World Championship in New Zealand, I returned to the world stage and ranked tenth after a less-than-desirable short program, trailing behind Simon and Paul in the top 8. My mom traveled to Auckland for the championship and was convinced that the timing of the cast removal from my broken arm the week prior had thrown me off completely. While I did lose some confidence, I attributed it more to nerves and over-ambition. Desperate to improve on my 1985 debut and make an impact, I realized I was out of my league, and my preparation reflected that.

1988 didn't improve much either. That year, the World Championships were held in Pensacola, Florida, marking my first trip to the United States. I prefer to tear out this page of my skating history book.

I was selected for second position on the team to compete in the men's free skating alongside Simon Reeves and David Morrison. At the time, I couldn't have expected to outperform my previous performances as I lacked the speed, confidence, and strength to match the technical brilliance of my competitors. Continuing to train at the youth hall wouldn't improve the situation anytime soon. My relationship with Mark was deteriorating rapidly. We frequently argued, and my frustration at being unable to perform elements I had mastered a year earlier was reaching its breaking point.

During one warm-up session, as I struggled with off-skate jumps, Mark, sitting on a milk crate and smoking a cigarette, vented his frustration by hurling the crate across the floor directly at me. After exchanging heated words, I stormed out of the rink, muttering,

" You're an asshole. "

Something had to dramatically change if I was going to reach the pinnacle for which I had so desperately strived. It plagued my thoughts—how, when, and what? These were questions to which I desperately sought answers.

The trip to Florida felt like a terrible waste of my parents' money, which didn't sit well with me. They had worked hard to send me overseas, and I felt I had squandered the opportunity. I couldn't wait to leave the US and return to Melbourne, where I was eager to attend a concert by my favorite band, Bros. In '88, Bros were topping charts worldwide (outside of the US) alongside another favorite of mine, Kylie Minogue. I was a die-hard fan of both, collecting every piece of memorabilia I could find—magazines, 12-inch singles, books, posters—you name it, I collected it all. I even had the Grolsch bottle top lids worn on Doc Marten shoes, the James Dean belt buckle, and a few pairs of ripped Levi 501s. Matt Goss, the band's lead singer, made these items must-haves in the late '80s, and I enthusiastically wore them. I even sported the 'Bros haircut,' a clipper fade with a slicked-back longer top.

They were the first live band I had ever seen and did not disappoint. I even went to see them at Luna Park in St Kilda, where they were filming a segment and appearing live on a Saturday morning music show. Two rows from the stage, I got my first glimpse of the stunning Goss twins in person. My friend Jason couldn't attend the concert at the last minute, so I invited young Simone instead. She loved singing and dancing, and although she wasn't a Bros fan then, she was eager to go. I jumped around and screamed along with everyone else at the gig, secretly wishing I could be on stage with them, even for a moment. Seeing Matt and the guys was a dream come true, and their music never failed to make me smile. Surrounded by screaming fans who idolized Bros, combined with my disappointing fourteenth-place finish in Florida, it sparked a much-needed change in my skating direction.

'No doubt you could become Australia's first World Champion.'

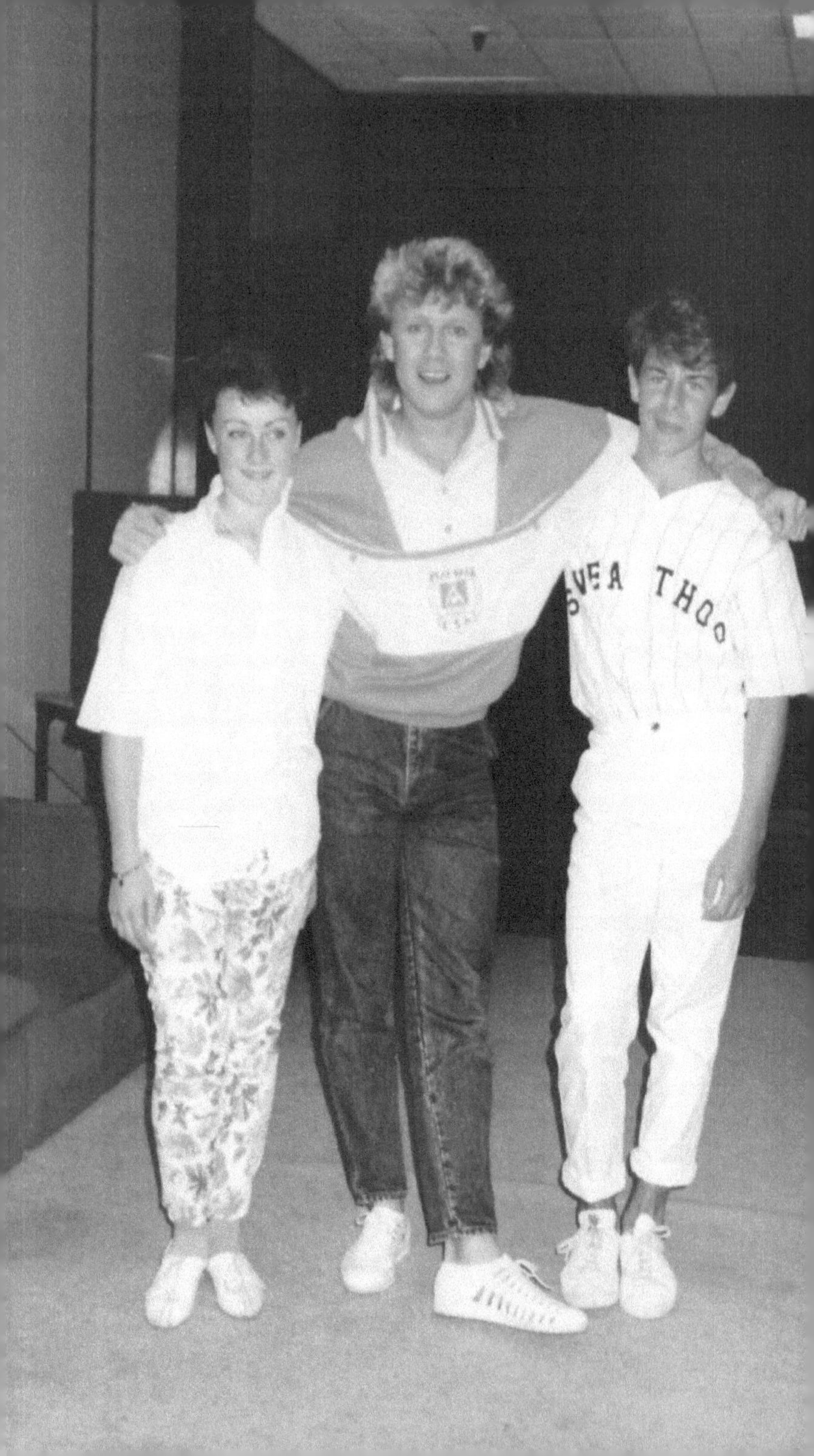

MOKING

Jason,

    Good luck in the future. I'm sure I'll see you around in Florida... Keep working!!

        Scott Cohen
        USA
        1987

6

THE BIG BREAK

Suddenly, I was infused with a new hunger to improve and the drive to propel me forward on the journey I longed for. As 1989 began, I approached it with a far more positive mindset. My training regimen intensified, fueled by a burning passion to succeed. Despite the challenges of the small youth center, my newfound determination was evident to everyone. I embraced the necessity of making the most of what I had to grow. My attitude became more focused and assertive, reflected in my skating choreography and overall lifestyle.

As I turned nineteen, I was eager to explore a more masculine approach to my long program, yearning for something distinctly different from my previous routines. Mark embraced the challenge and presented me with two unique programs, each paired with a bold choice of music. It felt like a great way to start the year afresh, especially after the past twelve months had been pretty awful.

I was still working at EBCO, and they continued to support my involvement in the sport, even if I wasn't succeeding. But I felt like I was finally back on track, and there were fewer times when I sat alone, battling back tears from a not-so-distant past. Those moments still haunted me when I thought about them too much.

In saying that, after the first few local competitions and mediocre performances, I soon reached a point where I realized I had grown significantly on all levels in recent years and that it was time to bid farewell to old baggage. It was time to move forward and strive for the heights I aspired to. I was tired of the monotonous routine and seeing no progress toward my goals. Despite training every day and putting in the hard work—or so I thought—the ups and downs began to wear on me, casting self-doubt. I knew that if I let this doubt creep in, I would end up where I was a year ago and possibly in the same place another twelve months down the line unless I made a change.

My parents supported me and worked just as hard to make this dream happen. They sacrificed many things to ensure my success, but I wasn't sure how long they could sustain this. How many more years could I keep chasing this dream at their expense? No doubt, they would have liked to enjoy holidays and other small luxuries around the house that they couldn't afford while I was skating, and it didn't feel fair.

> *When we bought our house, the carpet was old and worn out. We wanted to replace it, but we couldn't afford it while he was skating. Once Jayson finished school, started working, and began contributing financially, we gradually saved enough to buy the carpet after about ten years. We had to wait for all that to happen, after he reached his goals... Mom.*

It was time for me to shift gears. One fundamental aspect of this was navigating the limitations of my environment in the youth hall, but even more crucial was the decision to end the stagnant relationship with my coach. However, finding the courage to confront him was not yet on my list of newfound priorities. Don't get me wrong, I wanted to, but explaining that to my parents was also worrisome. I wasn't sure they would understand, and I feared that the conversation might bring up what happened in 1984 and that genie I wasn't about to let out of the bottle.

As if to shift my focus, an unexpected opportunity arose to compete at the World Games, which is considered the Olympic equivalent for all non-Olympic sports. Athletes, typically the top six to eight per event (excluding Figures) from each country, earn invitations based on their performance in the preceding World Championships. Held every four years, participation is a prestigious honor. Simon Reeves had been selected but chose to retire, leading to the invitation being extended to me. Somewhat of a gift, I might add. Despite immediate concerns about taking time off work, securing funds for travel to Europe, and managing various arrangements, I was ecstatic. I believed I had the strength to merit inclusion—this was an opportunity I was determined not to miss.

The World Games were held in Karlsruhe, Germany, just before the National Championships in Brisbane. It marked another first-time adventure for me and my first return to Europe since 1985. Our small team of five artistic skaters from Australia included me, David Morrison, Kirsten Murphy, Malcolm Bailey, and Tanya Davis (Malcolm and Tanya competed in the dance event). The atmosphere in town crackled with excitement, reminiscent of an Olympic Village. The festive spirit was fantastic, and the community's support was exceptional. Everyone we met in the streets was eager to extend their hospitality and help wherever possible.

Large audiences were a phenomenon I had only encountered previously in 1985 in Italy, where skating was immensely popular, and at the Expo. However, the crowds at the World Games surpassed anything I had witnessed before. On opening night, the stadium, which could hold five thousand at total capacity, was packed to standing room only. The audience appreciated every move of the performances. David and Kirsten made history for Australia by earning the country's first bronze medal for free skating pairs. Kirsten added to her success with a remarkable performance in the Ladies' free skating, where she held off Germany's Marina Keilman to claim another bronze, a first for Australia in that event. That being said, their success was overlooked entirely back home. Their achievements were not recognized, mainly Kirsten's two bronze medals. Instead, they became entangled in a dispute with the federation that nearly escalated to legal action at the national event just weeks later. We should have celebrated their success, and both skaters should have been inducted into the Hall of Fame for our sport.

On the contrary, I fell behind in my event, finishing fifth out of seven competitors. It was a disappointing result. Only eight skaters per event were invited to participate, so the fifth was not even halfway! Italy's Sandro Guerra proved too strong for David DeMotte of the USA, who took second place, while Germany secured the bronze. Despite my confidence in my preparation before the event, the competitiveness of the other skaters proved me wrong, prompting me to reassess my situation at home. It became evident that significant changes were necessary, and the time to make them was now—to move forward without dwelling on the past.

At nineteen years old, I had not achieved the goals I set for myself, including my dream of ranking in the top five at a world championship (excluding the World Games) within three years. There needed to be a functional relationship between Mark Lind and me, but there wasn't. My frustration was overwhelming. Once, I respected him as a coach, but that respect had long since faded in the haze of our strained relationship. I knew I couldn't confront him face-to-face to end our partnership; it was too complex. It would be fiery, and I would say what I wanted. Instead, I opted to write him a letter, the only way to express everything I needed him to understand.

I sought Colin's advice, finding him alone in the backyard shed. He appeared down but consumed as I was by the Mark situation; it didn't occur to me to ask how he was feeling. I just figured big brothers were always okay. I needed guidance, so I told him about my decision to leave my coach. Immediately, he expressed his dislike for the guy and admitted he might not be the best person to offer advice. Instead, he suggested I talk to Dad. And so, I did. His advice, as always, was straightforward:

> *Jay... Mark might be a great coach, but maybe not the right coach for you.*

Accompanied by my mother, we visited the youth hall in Sandringham for the last time, not to train but to deliver the letter to Mark. Mom stayed in the car while I entered the hall. Mary, busy making a cup of tea in the kitchen, could tell from my expression that the time had come. We'd talked about it a few times, but she always said, "When the time is right, you'll know it." She squeezed my hand and warned me he was in a foul mood.

I hadn't yet determined the direction of my skating future, but it was a pivotal moment for Mark and me as a team, evident when he entered the kitchen area. "Are you training or not?" he asked bluntly. I sat there trembling as he pulled out a cigarette and lit it. Summoning my courage, I stood and handed him the letter. He hesitated, shaking his head. "What's this?" he asked, exhaling a plume of smoke in my direction. "It's just easier this way," I replied nervously. He accepted it with a cold demeanor, muttering a few words. "Are you quitting?" he questioned. I shrugged my shoulders and stood firm. "We're over," I said, explaining that it was time for me to move on.

That brief interaction marked our last communication for years and the end of Mark's coaching career in Australia. He retired twenty-four hours later. It was a definitive break, lifting a significant burden off my shoulders and allowing me the space and time to reflect. I felt terrible for the skaters he left behind, especially the Milner girls, the Grigg family, Karen James and Karen Fraser. They were all great skaters. With few alternatives, some even quit skating altogether. It was a regrettable situation, and I felt selfish for contributing to it. It was one of those decisions you regret deeply. However, I never anticipated that my departure from the club would dramatically end Mark's involvement in the sport. Was it my fault? Or had he burned all his bridges?

After assessing my options and considering my situation, I contacted Simon Reeves for coaching. He was training a small group of skaters in Frankston and gladly agreed to assist me.

My first coach, Lynda, was still teaching at Roller City, and it was comforting to see her again and be in a familiar environment with her support. Our bond was profound and enduring, a connection I knew would last a lifetime, regardless of who else coached me. Unsure I would be welcomed back at the Club, I was pleasantly surprised by the warm reception following my departure from Mark. But reconnecting with old friendships happened quickly, and I felt a newfound freedom. Returning to a world-standard skating surface felt exhilarating. But that didn't last long, as he soon moved to another facility in Dandenong, which was even smaller than the youth club. This worried me, and I began to question my decision. Before long, we relocated to a larger rink, which was ideal, though nearly an hour away from home. It felt like a fresh start with a hint of direction. I was sure this was the path to follow... for now.

7

WHERE TO FROM HERE?

As preparations for the 1989 World Championships in Italy commenced, Elizabeth Bond, one of Mark's former top students, joined Simon's training group. Traveling from NSW to Melbourne for training brought back memories of our past collaborations and boosted our motivation before embarking on our journey to Europe. Liz, myself, and her sister Jillian, also a skater, had spent many great summers together. One unforgettable experience was at a NSW beach during a summer break. I went to visit the girls, and we decided to go swimming despite the red flags warning against it. Ignoring the danger, we plunged into the water and soon felt the sea's wrath, each of us having to be rescued by lifeguards.

ROLABOI, REVIVAL

> *Jayson, a few others, and I nearly drowned at South Shellharbour Beach one summer. We foolishly raced into a closed beach and a rip current, getting pulled about 100 meters out to sea. Seaweed tangled around our legs, making it a struggle to reach the shore, but we managed. To this day, we laugh about that near-death experience...*
> *LIZ BOND (Varga).*

Liz planned to compete in figure and free skating events. Still, she confided that she had been struggling with confidence lately and decided to prioritize the figure event at the championship. While I encouraged her to compete in free skating, I respected her decision, knowing her mental well-being was paramount.

> Nationals in 1989 were challenging for many of us skating under Mark Lind. Afterward, I declared that I would no longer compete in free skating. They still expected me to compete in Roccaraso, Italy, despite informing the Australian officials. I trained independently in Oak Flats with my sister Jillian's help before heading to Melbourne for lessons with Simon Reeves.
>
> Staying with Jayson, Bev, and Colin, their support was invaluable. I would not have gone to Worlds, even just for Figures, without Jayson's encouragement. Ultimately, I achieved my best result in a World Championship for figures...
> LIZ BOND (Varga).

Arriving in Milan, our team breezed through a minimal security check and boarded a forty-one-seater bus headed for our destination, Roccarasso, renowned as Southern Italy's premier resort for winter sports.

The journey onward was exhilarating as we climbed through crisp air along elevated roads hugging towering cliff faces. I avoided looking directly down from the bus window, feeling like I was ascending in an elevator along the side of a sixty-story building with a glass bottom.

In Roccarasso, my performances were average but represented a step in the right direction. Simon was a great supporter as our coach and put the fun back into competing, which Liz and I had missed over the past twelve months or more. I reclaimed a ranking among the top twelve and secured an overall eighth position in the combined Figures and Free skating division. The competition was electrifying, with Scott Cohen reclaiming his No. 1 title in a thrilling showdown. His battle with Sandro Guerra for the gold was intense, captivating the audience. The Italian spectators roared with support, creating an atmosphere akin to standing in the middle of a football field surrounded by twenty thousand screaming fans. Every moment of Sandro's routine held the crowd in suspense; they cheered with each successful element he completed. Despite Sandro's flawless performance, Scott Cohen clinched victory with a perfectly executed triple loop jump in his long program, securing the event's top spot.

Regardless of the results, one of the highlights of these competitions was forming new friendships abroad, and this trip was no different. I met a fantastic girl named Nicole Castellano from Illinois, USA, who skated pairs with her brother Paolo. Nicole and I remained friends after the championships, exchanging the most entertaining letters every week. Her mail always made me smile, and I'd worry if more than two weeks passed without hearing from her. Little did I know that my friendship with Nicole would soon challenge and reshape my understanding of myself in profound and unexpected ways. But that was still to come.

The year 1990 began with promise and hope, marked by yet another change of venue. Simon relocated to the Dandenong Showgrounds, where one of the large tin sheds typically reserved for sheep shearing exhibitions or cake stalls had been transformed by the roller hockey skaters and members of the Dandenong Club into a makeshift skating rink. The new setup featured a freshly laid cement floor, a barrier around the edge, and additional seating at one end for the parents. Though slightly larger than the hall used for Skate Connection, it was a significant downgrade from the huge rink we had been training at in Mooroolbark. However, its proximity to home meant I could quickly come and go after work, allowing for more training time.

Simon had gathered a large group of kids under his coaching, some of whom had moved across from Mark's team when he quit, while others were new recruits like Rachael Young. She was a cute little skater in the primary girls' category, showed immense promise and brimming with personality. She always clapped enthusiastically whenever I performed a triple jump near her or emerged from an inverted spin, her big brown eyes smiling at me through a dizzy haze.

> *As a 10-year-old, training on the same rink as Jayson was my first real understanding of what a great skater was. Initially, I was uncertain about sharing the floor with someone of his calibre. His speed, height, and grace amazed me, and I felt overwhelmed, especially since we were on such a small rink.*
>
> *However, these feelings quickly faded. Jay took me under his wing and taught me how to share the floor with him. As long as I held my line, my confidence grew, knowing Jay would always keep me safe and ensure we both executed our jumps and spins.*
>
> *Sometimes, this ended in a swinging hug as he finished a triple jump and I came out of an upright spin, centimeters apart. Little did I know, this was the beginning of a lifelong friendship...*
>
> RACHAEL YOUNG (SKETCHER)

The camaraderie among the team was undeniable. It was incredibly entertaining when a possum entered the building, or a bird flew through the open roller doors in the summer, causing a flurry of excitement. We often found vast amounts of rat and possum droppings on the rink each day, which we'd have to sweep up before starting skating. These quirky, unexpected moments made up for lacking a social life outside of work and training.

I needed to carefully consider my life away from the skating world, as my circle of friends was limited. I spent most of my free time with fellow skaters Jason Muscroft, Felicity Martin, Karen James, and Shane Grigg, enjoying movies or hanging out at each other's homes. Relationships weren't my priority then; I was happily single, and while I occasionally (rarely) went to clubs with friends, training commitments on Saturday and Sunday mornings were non-negotiable. As any athlete would attest, this dedication was essential for success—it demanded giving up a few luxuries. Ultimately, it boils down to your willingness to pay the price.

Luckily, another student at school understood the sacrifices needed for success. He was on the state cricket team and joked occasionally about his chances of playing for Australia. I was part of the national roller sports team, and he envied my inclusion. His name was Damien Fleming. He went on to have an impressive career as one of the great fast bowlers of our time. I wasn't following cricket closely, but around 1996, I saw him on the news and realized his success. It didn't surprise me; everyone at school feared facing his potent bowling that could knock you out in one go—another reason why I avoided sports class often. However, I had to face one of his bowls once, and it didn't end well.

The launch of the Oceania Games marked a significant turning point in my life. This international event, introduced outside the World Championships calendar, brought together athletes from the US, New Zealand, Australia, and China in Auckland in 1990. There, I met Charmaine, who would become my life's most influential and beautiful person.

Though we had crossed paths before, it was during this event that I truly got to know her and discovered her profound understanding of everything I questioned. Being with Charmaine gave me a sense of assurance and warmth that I had been missing since parting with my security blanket and dear friend, Lynda Flint. I was captivated by Charmaine and felt compelled to share my teenage experiences with her, confident that she would understand, though I couldn't bring myself to do so then.

Charmaine inspired me to believe in my potential for growth beyond my current state. Upon returning home from New Zealand, I eagerly planned a trip to Adelaide to see her. The anticipation leading up to the journey was almost overwhelming, filling me with excitement and nervousness, much to the disapproval of my mom, who believed I should stay home and focus on my training.

On the final evening in Auckland before heading home, an incident nearly jeopardized my competition status for a year. Late into the night, a sizable contingent of the Australian team was partying in one of the hotel rooms. Our accommodation overlooked a community garden filled with roses that reminded me of my mother's fondness. Beyond the garden, nestled among verdant hills, lay a hauntingly mysterious and seemingly forsaken cemetery.

The allure of a midnight excursion to this off-limits cemetery was irresistible. As we celebrated in the hotel room, curiosity got the better of us, and I found myself unable to resist joining the others in crossing the road. Laughter and shrieks echoed from the park as we approached this intriguing destination. It was past 11:30 PM, enveloped in darkness that felt straight out of a Hollywood thriller: the eerie valley, weathered tombstones, chilling fog, unsettling cries of nocturnal creatures, and only the faint glow of moonlight to guide us.

It turned into quite an adventure, albeit a nerve-wracking one. I half-expected a homicidal maniac to leap out from behind a tombstone and threaten us all. The reality was almost as alarming: a booming, authoritative voice in the distance, instantly recognizable as our Federation President, Ivan Martin. My heart sank. The game was up, and we scattered like startled mice in that panic.

Assuming me to be the ringleader, Ivan called out my name angrily, his face a mask of fury. I knew I was in serious trouble.

> *"Jayson Sutcliffe! ... Get over here!"*

My first thought was, 'I'm done for.'

Nearby, Jennifer Milner and the others fled in fear of being implicated. I reassured a terrified Shane Grace that I would take full responsibility. It offered little solace, however, as Ivan's reprimand was severe and unrelenting. Defeated, we all trudged back to the hotel, heads low.

Even Gail Collier, the US coach, struggled to maintain a stern demeanor as her son Courtney and his partner Eryn were among those caught. As we silently chuckled at our predicament on the walk uphill, the relief of returning to the relative safety of our rooms was short-lived. The incident was swept under the rug until the next day when a meeting was convened to face the consequences. Unexpectedly, during the meeting, I was publicly informed that the Federation intended to impose an immediate 12-month suspension on me. They cited my role as the adult in the group and my perceived allowance for the incident. I couldn't believe it—everyone else received warnings, yet I bore the total penalty. They were exerting their authority and using me as a scapegoat.

It appeared to continue its efforts to penalize me for the Skate Connection club's collapse, which occurred after Mark Lind abandoned it following my departure. Many within the sport's hierarchy had previously entrusted Mark with coaching their daughters, leading to the club's demise. The pieces fell into place.

Fortunately, strong support from John Brogan and the Dandenong RS Club in the following months prevented the National body from enforcing the suspension. A hearing at the 1990 National Championships reduced the suspension to a probationary period and a substantial fine.

Back to Charmaine. In the middle of the year, I packed my car and embarked on the 790 km road trip to Adelaide to visit this amazing woman who had completely turned my world around. She had invited me for the weekend, and despite the long eight-hour drive straight from work on a Friday afternoon, I was eager not only to see her and Ali (Charmaine's equally vibrant and fun friend who shared a passion for fashion design) but also to experience my first independent interstate journey driving my car.

Arriving quite late, any exhaustion from the journey dissolved as adrenaline surged upon meeting Charmaine. Ali was busy sewing an outfit for the night out, and I eagerly joined in to help. They were headed to a club, which caught me off guard, but being in Adelaide and embracing a new experience, I was up for it.

Training commenced, and I began to spread my wings. While I appreciated the attention from younger skaters Amanda and Tammy Bryant, the bond with Charmaine held the most significance for me. I felt a youthful excitement when we ventured out to a warehouse party—something entirely new. I held her hand throughout the night, feeling nervous and excited. I refrained from drinking much, though I couldn't ignore the presence of a few gorgeous guys around my age, which stirred up my hormones. Ali inadvertently asked,

> *"Do you have a boyfriend, Jazzie?"*

It caught me completely off guard and nearly caused me to spit my drink over the other partygoers. I dodged the question and started to dance, albeit not that well.

Despite feeling strongly connected with Charmaine, I wasn't ready to openly share my truth. She was the one I wanted to confide in, believing she would accept and understand me unconditionally. Yet, finding the courage to do so remained frustratingly out of reach. If only I could have mustered the strength to reveal my inner turmoil.

Looking back, it was incredibly naive of me to think that most people I knew hadn't already figured out I was gay. None of them would have cared. Why I tried to hide it, I'm not sure. It just didn't feel right to accept or publicize it fully. My sexuality remained a private part of my life, one that I didn't fully understand beyond my own experiences. I worried about how my parents would react, though deep down, I suspected they already had a clue. I often reminisce about when my mother discovered a few letters under my mattress. I had exchanged these letters with my interstate friend, whom I was so in love with, or so I thought. Upon reading them, she confronted me angrily one day after school, demanding to know if I was gay. In a panic, I lied immediately, snatched the letters from her, and fled to our yard. There, I tearfully burned every letter in the incinerator.

Before I knew it, dawn broke, leaving only a few hours until our next training session. The weekend in Adelaide flew by all too quickly, and saying goodbye was tough. Those two days with Charmaine felt like an eternity, not because they dragged on but because they enveloped me in a warm cocoon of love and possibility.

Two weeks later, I returned to Adelaide, and shortly afterward, I made the difficult decision to part ways with Simon, my coach up until that point. He was understanding and supportive, encouraging me to pursue what was best for my skating career. Simon had been an invaluable motivator and close friend during the ten months we worked together, but the opportunity to train under Charmaine offered a new dimension. I relocated to the Skateworld Noble Park rink to begin this new chapter.

Trips to Adelaide became more frequent, and I was grateful that Charmaine also flew over occasionally to work with me. The training became intense, and my goals became clear. She introduced a rigorous new training program that pushed me to my limits and revamped my routines with elements I had never imagined attempting before. Everything started falling into place beautifully.

> *I remember Jayson coming over frequently to train and have lessons with our coach, Charmaine. I used to love it when he would come and train with us. It would always make me step it up a level and show off to try and impress him, never knowing if I ever did, of course... AMANDA BRYANT*

My parents made a rare appearance at one of my last training sessions. Mom was wearing the new tracksuit I made for her, turquoise and white pants, and a jacket set she loved and wore often. Dad arrived with his video camera poised to capture the action. I felt nervous but eager to showcase what I had been diligently working on. My mom, always my harshest critic, was already on the sideline, anxious to see what I had to offer. It was their first meeting with Charmaine, and Dad greeted her with a playful question:

> "What have you done to my boy, Charmaine?"

Her response brought a smile to my face. "He's not a boy anymore, Colin."

As I effortlessly executed my triple jumps on the rink, I caught sight of my mom. Tears welled in her eyes, and she clasped her hands close to her mouth, clearly moved and proud. Skating over to her, slightly breathless, I intended to hug her, but she reached out and wrapped her arms around Charmaine instead. Dad, setting down his camera, patted me on the back and looked at Charmaine, saying,

> "You've given him wings."

Feeling overwhelmed, I fought back tears and performed my short program for them to enjoy. I'd found my path. It was a defining moment. I felt that everything I had worked for, desperately wanted to achieve, and was capable of was evident. I could see that Mom and Dad now believed our dream would come true.

8

THIS TIME I KNOW IT'S FOR REAL

Within two months, we were gearing up to compete on the world stage, this time in Hanau, Germany. For the first time, it dawned on me that I could truly contend among the best. The 1990 World Meet loomed ahead, and I was more than prepared. This championship held a special significance for me, unlike any other before it. It was my 'Rocky' moment. I'd worked my ass off, paid my dues, and was ready to roll.

For years, I aimed to break into the elite ranks of world athletes, harboring a distant hope that one day I might match their brilliance. The challenge had always been my lack of confidence and support. This time was different. A master plan was in motion, and deep inside, I no longer aspired to be like the others—I wanted to beat them. This shift in mindset was catalyzed by my newfound determination, fueled in part by motivational and self-help literature. These books opened my eyes to the negativity that had held me back, transforming my thoughts into positive actions.

In the early days of training in Hanau, there was a buzz among skaters about "the guy from down under," a 20-year-old newcomer who had suddenly emerged as a serious contender. Though I had been in the sport for years, I had never been seen as such a threat. It was both daunting and exhilarating. Surprisingly, Italy's leading man, Sandro Guerra, was a 'no show' due to an injury. While this was hugely disappointing for Italy and Sandro, it meant another door had opened and an opportunity I could only try to monopolize. When the time came to perform my short program, the first of two at the event, I felt the anticipation in the air.

Clad in a black costume with a controversial glove attached to one sleeve—previously frowned upon by Mom and judges at Nationals—this time was different. My teammate Stuart Popplewell was the skater before me in the competition. It was his debut at the world championship, and unfortunately, things hadn't gone well for him. I empathized with his feelings, having experienced similar disappointments after a poor performance. However, I shifted my focus entirely to my own game.

Standing on the sidelines, I shook my legs and glanced back at Charmaine. She squeezed my hand reassuringly and urged me to

" *"Just do it."* "

ROLABOI, REVIVAL

I stepped onto the rink with an eerie calm, fully aware that this moment was crucial—now or never.

Every element I performed garnered applause, and I felt a sense of ease wash over me. Inside, I couldn't help but smile. It marked the first time I had cleanly landed a triple flip in competition. Over two minutes, I squeezed in four triple jumps, a double axel, and two spins. My heart raced with an intense, primal passion that fueled my performance. Mom would have been jumping for joy.

My performance in the short program was nearly flawless, leaving spectators pondering the source of this sudden transformation. Thankfully, given my slender physique, concerns about doping or drug use were unfounded. Tests at the championship also put that rumor to bed.

When the scores were announced, I was astounded. I had never received scores higher than 5.6, but this time, they ranged from 5.7 to 5.9 across the board. It was clear—I had broken into the top tier, possibly even the top five. In that exhilarating moment, I threw myself into Charmaine's arms and waved enthusiastically at my team in the stands. It was a truly iconic moment, and I asked myself, "Was this for real?"

Later, we stood anxiously in the upper stands, waiting nervously for the results to be posted on the notice board. As the crowd gathered around the list, I heard gasps of surprise. I hurried over to see for myself and was stunned to discover that I had secured third place, with Scott Cohen in second, among a formidable field of competitors. This was an unprecedented achievement for an Australian. I was eager to share the news with my family back home, but my parents were out when

I called, so I spoke with my brother, Colin, instead. He was thrilled upon hearing the news, though he didn't realize I still had to complete my final program to secure the medal. His happiness for me was palpable in his voice.

The mental exhaustion of competing at such a high level was overwhelming. While I had participated in several world meets, this one felt distinctly different. Perhaps it was the adrenaline-fueled excitement or the laser-sharp focus that drained me, or maybe a combination of both. That night, sleep eluded me as I feared my chances of a Top 3 ranking could slip away.

Fortunately, the morning of the final got off to a great start. Charmaine and I were sitting together on the bus. "It's gonna be a good day, Jazzie," she said confidently. She had noticed on the clock that it was 11:11, and it was the ultimate sign. Those few words were enough for me.

Watching the official training for the top group of men on the last day of competition at a world meet is always a highlight, and this time, for the first time, I was in it. David DeMotte from the USA won the short program, with Scott Cohen in second after a fall on his triple loop jump. Yes, I was sitting behind my childhood hero, Scott Cohen. Stuff dreams are made of. David, a tall and solidly built guy, had a few problems training with more complex elements, making me think he must be struggling with the intensity, too. In contrast, Italy's Patrick Venerucci looked very strong. He was breathing down our necks, making for fierce competition.

It wasn't long before we found ourselves back in the arena, preparing for battle. My costume for the night was simple: all black, with light chiffon strips from the shoulders in the form of tangled leaves. I was skating to music selections by George Winston, Mendelssohn, and Puccini's Madame Butterfly. It was a strange combination, but they were my favorite pieces, and the choreography was simple.

The skaters in the top group before me performed strongly, although a few made errors. I felt the adrenaline surge through my body like never before. Charmaine stood calmly beside me, holding my hand. Scott Cohen was only a few feet away with his headphones on, and eyes closed. As soon as I took my position on the rink, waiting for my music to start, I froze in anticipation.

> *God, I prayed, don't let me fuck this up.*

It was silent. I could almost hear my heart beating. Then, the music began. As soon as I listened to the first note of George Winston's "Spring," I felt a sudden rush of warmth and calm. I felt unstoppable after completing my first element perfectly—a triple toe loop. But lining up for my triple flip jump, I knew this was the make-or-break moment. I had to nail this jump. As I took off into the air, one, two, three rotations, and landed cleanly on one foot, the exhilaration was intoxicating, and my smile was as wide as the skating surface. The roar of the crowd lifted me beyond my imagination. Four minutes might not sound like a long time, but under the spotlight, it can feel like an eternity of pure ecstasy.

The final position in my program had me arched back, rolling down the center of the floor with my arm stretched toward the ceiling. I clenched my fist at the final extension and whispered, "You've done it." That was all I could have asked of myself as pride, joy, and relief swelled inside me. Charmaine was waiting for me rink side with open arms. We fell into each other and hugged with such intense emotion I thought I might burst.

I remember how the cup of water she was holding for me spilled all over my shoulder and down my back as we embraced. We laughed about it, even though it was the least of our concerns in that moment of excitement.

We sat nervously before the cameras on the makeshift stage beside the rink, awaiting the judge's decision. I was shaking so much that I could barely hold the cup of water, let alone drink from it. A sudden roar from the crowd confirmed the good news. We stood up to look at the digital display, staggered to see my lowest score was 5.7 (out of 6) and my highest was 5.9. The second mark for Manner of Performance was also 5.7 to 5.9. "Stoked" is the only word that comes to mind.

At that point, I was leading the competition, and the thought in my head was, "I'm in the lead at a world championship!" Just as Jason Muscroft turned to me with a cheeky smile and said,

> "Do you realize you're in the fucking lead right now?"

We laughed, even though he was right. Reality was sinking in. There were only a few skaters left, and it meant I was almost guaranteed a medal. I was shaking at the thought. To think, I was in the lead, chasing the one and only Scott Cohen... but it was only for a short time. Scott had yet to take the floor, and when he did, his performance was phenomenal. As soon as he opened with a perfectly executed triple loop, I knew the crown would be his. Triple after triple after triple, performed effortlessly. He took the gold from Davide DeMotte, who had been leading the short program.

Nonetheless, I clinched the silver, and Italy's Patrick Venerucci climbed into third. It was the first time an Australian athlete had won an individual medal in a single event, not a combination of events. Previously, we had a medalist in the men's combined event, Paul Irving, and I was blown away by that achievement. We were all filled with tears and had plans for a big celebration back at the hotel. I knew our managers, Ian, Anne and Rosemary, would be cracking out the bubbly.

It might have "only" been silver, but to us, it was gold.

JAYSON SUTCLIFFE

> *In 1990, I knew that things had changed. I think the tide had changed a little bit for Jayson and me. Jayson was a young kid, and I was this established, seasoned athlete, like the veteran, and he was the novice who was coming up, so there was a lot of space between the novice and the expert.*
>
> *Then he started to come up, and you know, his abilities grew and, and then it was more like we were real. At one time, we became very competitive with each other, so the dynamics of our relationship changed, and at that point in 1990, when I won, and he got second, I could see that Jayson had crossed over a line, a very appropriate line to cross, but the relationship had changed. I think he still admired me, but now he was after me...* SCOTT COHEN

It was uncanny that only six years prior, I had met Scott Cohen at a training seminar in Adelaide, held at the same rink where Charmaine was now teaching me. Standing alongside Scott as the World Silver medalist was a surreal moment I will remember for the rest of my life.

I wished my parents could have been with me in Germany. Mom would've been overjoyed, and Dad, well, he'd have said, "You ripper, Jay." I couldn't wait to get on the phone and tell them the results. My mother cried before I even finished telling her. I could hear her voice trembling and could picture her teary-eyed and shaking. It was just as much my parents' dream to see me on the podium as mine. We had all worked so hard over the past eight years to make it happen that the medal deserved to be around their necks, too.

I slept with my medal on my bedside table that night because I couldn't believe it was mine to keep. Back at the hotel, Rosemary Wilkins and Anne Bond cracked open the champagne and told me that Anne had spoken to Mark Lind on the phone to inform him of the result. I wasn't sure how to feel about that; I didn't want it to seem like we were rubbing it in his face. Or did I? Anne said he couldn't believe it, as it was just over a year ago that we had parted, and I was still ranked fourteenth.

Anne and Rosemary also coordinated the numerous faxes from supporters and well-wishers back home while sending out many of their own. They couldn't understand why I wasn't out celebrating with the rest of the team, but I wasn't in the mood to burn up the dance floor or drink myself to oblivion. I was still slightly shocked and happy to wait until the next night's closing banquet to let loose.

The team parted ways on the final day in Hanau, each traveling separately back to Australia. I traveled by train to Milan with Charmaine and Nadine Lewis, a former skater I had admired as a youngster in Melbourne. We had an incredible time in Italy before I explored London alone. I hoped to find some cool shoes and a few rare 12-inch records, ideally by Kylie, Madonna, or Bros, that I wouldn't have been able to return home. I spent most of my time scurrying around Soho and venturing up and down Oxford Street, soaking in the London style before returning to Australia. As I was looking through HMV, the UK Top 40 was being played in-store, and I vividly recall the intro: "In at number two, it's Kylie Minogue, with a new one, Step Back in Time." I couldn't contain myself; I'd never heard the song before and burst into a spontaneous dance.

I met up with a fellow skater, Paul Whitaker, who was in London. It was great to see him, and he urged me to see "Starlight Express." As an avid fan of musicals, I took his advice, and thankfully so. The show was incredible. I had seen it earlier in Australia, but that was an arena spectacular, and this version was a knockout. Given that the show was performed entirely on roller skates, it made me ponder a future on wheels in a different direction. However, that idea was short-lived since I couldn't sing a note to save my life.

I had hoped my arrival in Melbourne would be low-key, but as I walked through the customs door, I was staggered to see a crowd with banners. It was even more surprising (and a bit embarrassing) that they were ringing cowbells! My parents were there, of course. Mom couldn't contain her happiness, bursting into tears when she saw me, while Dad smiled proudly. It was a wonderful surprise, capping off the trip in a way that genuinely made me feel special.

I was stunned and excited to see my older brother, Colin, there. He stood tall in the background, arms crossed, silently acknowledging his pride in our shared joy. Colin and I never had much in common, but he always looked out for me, especially in primary school. He was a bit of a lady's man, which always impressed me, and despite our differences, we maintained a good relationship. As with all my family, I couldn't imagine life without him. He always kept things real and wasn't shy about calling me out if I was being difficult.

During the Christmas break that year, work closed for a few weeks, and I decided to travel to Los Angeles to visit some of my new skating friends. I arranged to stay with Nicky Armstrong, a former World Pairs Champion. The idea of being in California and training at a few of the local rinks excited me to no end. Many skaters I had met at previous World Championships lived and trained in California, and I couldn't wait to catch up with a few of them. Arriving in L.A. wasn't without a hiccup either. I was pretty sick on the flight over, possibly something I ate, and when we landed, I was still in the lavatory, dealing with intense nausea. It was so overwhelming that I didn't even realize the plane had stopped until the cleaners pushed open the door, surprised to find me still inside.

As I staggered off the plane and into an empty arrivals area, I saw Nicky standing with her mom. They were about to leave and were shocked to see me in such a state. "Welcome to L.A.," I thought to myself.

My illness persisted, keeping me confined to bed for the first few days. It was torture not being able to venture out and skate. Little did I expect Nicky to receive a call from the organizers of an exhibition in Italy inviting her to participate. Before I knew it, Nicky had told them I was with her, and the invitation was also extended to me. Heading to Europe on this trip was beyond my wildest dreams—fantastic!

In New York, we reunited with the rest of the team: Paolo and Nicole Castellano, Susie Heck, Doug Wait, and Deanna Monahan, all skilled skaters. During the flight, Nicole tried to give me a crash course in Italian, her native tongue. We spent most of the journey laughing, feeling fortunate to be brought back together by fate.

Following a hugely successful show in Roseto, we boarded a bus with the Bologna Roller Skating Club, embarking on a five-and-a-half-hour drive through snowy landscapes under the night sky. Upon arriving in Bologna and checking into Hotel Regina, near Agosto Square, I found myself inexplicably fascinated, perhaps infatuated, with Nicole. It was a thrilling discovery because until then, I had been sure of my attraction to men and had accepted that I was gay! Yet suddenly, I was drawn to this stunning woman with Broadway-worthy looks. But it wasn't just her appearance—but her ability to make me laugh and smile like no one else could. I could only chalk it up to "chemistry."

I might have started flirting with her, but I wasn't entirely sure I was doing it right. With her older brother, skating partner, and guardian Paolo always around, any potential for more fizzled out quickly, along with any notion of exploring heterosexuality. New Year's Eve celebrations and a birthday party for one of the skaters in Bologna passed without me delving further into these new, unfamiliar feelings.

Nicole, Jayson & Deanna.

Instead, upon returning to Melbourne, my focus shifted to another woman—Kylie Minogue. Her 'Enjoy Yourself' Tour was about to hit the stage at the Rod Laver Arena, and I was buzzing with excitement—not just about seeing Kylie but also about what I'd be wearing. I decided to stick with my staple ripped Levi 501s and a sleeveless hooded tee, but I added a personal touch: large felt cut-out letters spelling "Kylie 'What Do I Have to Do?'" attached to the back of my shirt and down the side of my jeans, with a Kylie logo and a few red love hearts on the front. I was so pumped to wear this outfit; it was a hit at the show. People stopped me everywhere, wanting to take photos, and I felt part of the spectacle.

JAYSON SUTCLIFFE

> " *I remember every year at worlds walking into Jayson's room and seeing various pictures of celebrities on the wall. Most of the time, it was always Kylie—he was just obsessed with her. You'd walk in and see her pictures everywhere...* "
> TAMMY BRYANT

My first live experience seeing Kylie was at the Cadillac Bar, a precursor to her live shows and an incredibly intimate event that wasn't advertised as Kylie but as the 'Singing Budgie,' the unfortunate tag the press had given her. I attended this special gig with Simon Reeves, and her boyfriend, Michael Hutchence, was there too, cheering her on as she belted out the hits. The atmosphere was electric, and you wouldn't get this personal experience at an arena show—the fans were ecstatic.

But the real magic happened after the show. Simon and I lingered backstage, hoping to catch a glimpse of Kylie. To our delight, she appeared with Michael and her manager, Terry Blamey. Kylie signed an autograph and was incredibly friendly, chatting with us as if we were old friends. Remarkably, no one else was there—just us. As they got into Terry's Mercedes Benz to leave, Michael, ever the rockstar, opened the window, stuck his head out, and waved at us. Then, in a final rockstar gesture, he tossed an empty bottle out the window. We couldn't stop laughing and were utterly blown away by what happened.

I have been arguably one of Kylie's biggest fans since I

first saw her on The Sullivans, playing the role of a Dutch girl named Carla. That feels like a lifetime ago, around 1979! Her ongoing success and evolving artistic directions over the years captivated me, turning me into a devoted fan.

You have to admire Kylie's journey to stardom. She's faced criticism from all sides and always looked back with a smile. Today, she's reached an iconic status that can't be undone. I adore her.

My room became a 'Kylie' shrine for many years.

So, am I gay or not? I couldn't deny my feelings for Nicole, although I never acted on them, and I love Kylie (though let's not take that too seriously). The answer to my question came at a significant turning point in my life: when Madonna released her movie 'Truth or Dare' (re-titled in Australia as 'In Bed with Madonna'). It was a testament to the profound impact of pop culture on our lives. The sheer flamboyancy of the all-male dancers, paired with their over-the-top costumes and behavior, pushed every boundary. It gave me the confidence to embrace my sexuality. Many of Madonna's entourage were openly gay and apologetically proud, and I finally acknowledged that this was the world fate had chosen for me.

Would you believe I saw that movie at least twelve times in the cinema with my best friend, Shannon Ferris? It became almost a ritual for us to watch it every Tuesday!

Only a few close friends knew about my sexual orientation, Shannon being one of the first, and she always encouraged me to find a 'boyfriend,' which wasn't on the agenda. But it seemed to be common knowledge within the sport. I often heard derogatory terms like 'Poofter' and 'faggot', especially at National meets where all four disciplines of the sport converged. Speed and Hockey skaters mainly held animosity towards many of us in Artistic skating. At the same time, a few good eggs respected us as athletes and treated us no differently.

After performing at a competition in Brisbane, I skated off the floor to await my scores, and flowers and small gifts were thrown onto the rink, which initially seemed nice. It was only when I picked them up that I looked down in horror, only to find two condoms filled with 'Chomp' chocolate bars and a note reading 'poofter.' I suspect a group of Hockey skaters threw this 'gift,' and I wondered if they understood how ignorant and hurtful their actions were.

During the 1991 Australian Championships in Homebush, Sydney, SBS Television expressed interest in featuring me in a story they were doing at the event. When the crew arrived, they seemed somewhat surprised by the high skill level displayed in the sport. I'm not sure what they expected, but they were impressed by what they saw. Amanda and Tammy Bryant even took it upon themselves to teach the interviewer how to skate. He was using roller hockey skates and, for someone who had never skated before, he wasn't half bad.

We set up the camera on the floor during the filming to capture close-up shots and dynamic angles. At one point, I was performing footwork directly towards the camera lens. The closing shot was supposed to show me scissoring over the top of the camera and gliding over the cameraman lying on the floor. You guessed it—I slipped and collided straight into the camera during the final scissor maneuver. Aside from being incredibly embarrassed, I was terrified that I had damaged a camera lens worth about two thousand dollars. Thankfully, no actual harm was done—phew!

After a lengthy interview, the crew waited until late evening to film the event I was competing in, Senior Men's. I debuted my Edward Scissorhands-inspired program nationally to an enthusiastic audience. This was a dramatic departure, as I typically performed classical pieces. Danny Elfman's music, dark and mysterious with hypnotic choral vocals, captivated me deeply. Its epic storytelling nature resonated with me, and including three triple jumps delighted the audience. At the request of the film crew, I performed the routine again for filming purposes. Despite being late, to my delight, most of the audience stayed till the end.

Following the SBS feature, another of my skating contacts offered me a spot on a popular Australian show called 'That's Dancin'. The show was thriving, known for its weekly contests among top ballroom dancers (pre-dating 'Strictly Ballroom' fame). I joined a small group of Victorian skaters and four roller dance teams to perform. We choreographed a tight routine to a piece from 'A Chorus Line.' Despite the limited floor space, our performance was entertaining and successful—but without its challenges...

The show occurred in front of a theater-style audience, and our performance was scheduled midway through the program. We didn't anticipate that the dancers had the floor regularly waxed. Let me tell you, wax and wheels do not mix well! Our introduction turned into a cringe-worthy disaster. The wax made the floor incredibly slippery, making it nearly impossible for us to stay upright, let alone perform our routine. Everything came to a grinding halt only a minute into our performance.

In a frantic rush, the crew hastily spread generous amounts of Ajax powder on the surface to give us some traction. When we took the stage an hour later, the floor resembled more of an ice rink than a dance floor. We had one shot to nail the performance, and that we did.

9

YOU LEFT US SO SUDDENLY

Following a training trip to Adelaide to visit Charmaine, my life was about to take another unexpected turn. The night before my departure, I ventured alone to Three Faces, a club in Melbourne. Earlier, I had argued with my mom over my outfit—a new tight black Lycra mesh top I had made, paired with black jeans and a touch of eyeliner. She was concerned about my dedication to skating, as the world championship in Sydney is fast approaching. After a heated exchange, she stormed off to her room, leaving me frustrated, while Dad sat in his armchair with Coco, our beautiful cat, sitting comfortably on his knee. He didn't have much to say, but I knew what he was thinking. I 'accidentally' slammed the front door and stepped outside into the cold of night, only to almost step over Colin, who was perched on the front step. He'd been drinking, and his words were slurred, but he wanted to know I was okay. He asked, "You havin' a night out with the boys?"

I wasn't sure how to interpret that, but I think he understood where I was. Sadly, I didn't comprehend his.

I was nervous as I walked through the club, feeling at home and like an outsider. Among the smoke-filled air, I exchanged glances with a handsome Mediterranean guy. Spontaneously, he took my hand and pulled me onto the dance floor. Butterflies surged through me, just like the first time I put on my skates. There was a brief sense of familiarity before he unexpectedly kissed me, and soon, we were writhing on the dance floor, as if it were meant to be, to the Kylie track, 'What Do I Have to Do?'

Later, Troy and I left the club and walked across the street to the local supermarket, which fortunately was open 24/7. A few hoon drivers circled the area in a beat-up car, their shouts echoing in the night. I didn't realize they were targeting us until I felt a sharp slap on the back of my neck, followed by another. Reaching behind my head, I discovered we had been hit with eggs just as the drivers shouted,

> Go home, you faggots.

That was enough for me, and I was done for the night.

I overslept that morning and returned home late. My mom woke me up with a pillow to my head, reminding me that "this is not a hotel." She also warned me to hurry up or risk missing my flight to Adelaide, which I had forgotten. My brother Colin, who usually just dropped me off at the terminal entrance, surprised me by walking to the departure gate to say goodbye. It seemed unusual, but I understood he struggled after recently ending a long-term relationship. He didn't want to talk about it, and I didn't know what to say either. As he left, I joked, "Don't speed in my car, okay?" "Nah, she'll be right, Jay. See you, mate," he chuckled in response. I didn't look back at him, but I knew he was watching me leave.

I loved being in Adelaide until one evening, cruising around town in Ali's quaint old Volkswagen, we encountered a car that had hit a large dog. The injuries were severe, prompting us to act swiftly. Carefully, we placed the dog in the car's back seat and rushed to the nearest veterinary clinic. I vividly recall the weight of sadness, realizing the tragic nature of the situation. It's astounding how deeply death can affect you, even when it involves a life you weren't directly connected to. I couldn't help but imagine the devastation I would feel if it were a family member or friend. Within minutes, it was clear that the dog couldn't be saved despite our efforts.

Training in Adelaide this time was starkly different from my usual trips, where I felt exhilarated and determined. Instead, I was frustrated, out of shape, and consumed by fear—fear that I wouldn't be able to replicate my success from 1990, fear of disappointing my mom, and failing to meet expectations in front of a hometown crowd at the upcoming world event. Charmaine reminded me that "I had nothing to prove to anyone" and that skating for myself was the most important thing to do now. She was right, once again. I had lost touch with the very reasons I laced up my skates every day of the year. The thrill of gliding on the rink, the rush of performing in front of an audience, the sheer joy and exhilaration of every movement—I had forgotten it all. Instead, I was consumed by the pressure to meet others' expectations, become the person they wanted me to be, and win the accolades they craved. In the process, I neglected my dreams, passions, and what truly made me come alive. I had lost sight of what I loved and wanted, buried beneath the weight of others' desires. It was time to break free from this rut and refocus on what mattered. I needed to reignite the fire within and get back in the game with renewed determination. The road ahead wouldn't be easy, but I was ready to embrace the challenge ahead in Sydney. It was time to skate for myself again.

Upon arriving in Melbourne, my father and younger brother, Shane, were waiting at the airport to pick me up. There was an eerie silence as we walked back to the car. It wasn't like my dad to be so quiet, and I sensed something was wrong. As I settled into the passenger's seat and buckled my seat belt, my father sadly looked at me. Glancing over my shoulder, I noticed tears streaming down Shane's face.

"It's about Colin," my father began, his voice trembling.

" He's taken his life. "

The news of my brother's death hit me with a shocking and numbing force simultaneously. It felt like the ground had vanished beneath me. Learning that he had taken his own life blurred reality into a hazy fog. Dad reached over and put his hand on my shoulder, a gentle gesture of comfort amid our shared grief. I could hear Shane sniffling softly in the backseat, each sniffle a poignant reminder of our pain. Unable to face them, I turned away and looked out the window, the world outside a blur through my tear-filled eyes.

Had I missed something? There were no signs that I could recall indicating he might do something like this. How did I fail to notice? I couldn't decide whether to cry or remain composed. My mind raced with overwhelming thoughts: frustration, anger, fear, and a profound sense of emptiness. I rolled down the window, desperately trying to absorb the gravity of this news with a deep breath of air.

"Who found him and where," I managed to ask, dreading the answer. I prayed it wasn't my mother who discovered my brother's lifeless body.

"Your mother did," Dad replied softly, his voice barely above a whisper. The words hung in the air, heavy with unspoken emotions and memories. His eyes held a mixture of sadness and understanding, and I could feel the weight of the truth settling in, deepening the ache in my heart.

But anger surged through me when I learned it was her. At that moment, I hadn't paused to consider the pain my brother must have been enduring. I was overwhelmed with frustration that he had inflicted such anguish on Mom. She had already faced similar pain in the past, and I knew this would trigger painful memories and potentially set back her progress in overcoming earlier bouts of depression. The thought of her reliving those dark times, grappling with the heavy burden of grief once more, filled me with a sense of helpless anger. It wasn't just about my sorrow but the fear of seeing her shattered again after all the strength and years it had taken her to rebuild.

For a fleeting moment, the world around me seemed unreal as I stared out the window at the passing scenery. When we approached home, I could no longer contain my tears. I wanted my father to see me as strong, so I tried suppressing my emotions. But in the silence of my despair, tears silently streamed down my cheeks as I buried my face in my hands.

When I saw my mother hunched over in her chair, her pain and heartbreak were palpable. Images of the events from the past days flashed through my mind with a mix of fear and sadness. The devastation in her eyes was undeniable. I had no words to comfort her grief. Yet, as we embraced, I felt a release—a sense that my presence could somehow ease her burden. It was as though my return marked the final stage of her immediate grieving process, knowing that I had come home to share in her sorrow.

I was the last in our family to learn of Colin's death, and for that, I was grateful. I couldn't bear receiving such devastating news while still in South Australia, far from home. But now, I faced the daunting task of relaying the news to Charmaine. I broke down completely when I heard her voice, unable to hold back the flood of emotions. It was as if she already knew what had happened, sensing the gravity of my silence and the tremble in my voice. We didn't say much, but knowing she was there, on the other end of the line, offered a small but significant comfort amidst the overwhelming grief.

I sat outside in the spot Colin had chosen as his final place: our family garage, where we all parked our cars. He loved his cars and was known as a 'rev head' who loved his Johnny Walker. It would remain a poignant reminder of the tragic loss we endured for years to come. As tears streamed down my face, I sat there, partly wanting to be alone with my grief and partly wanting to console my devastated mother, who knelt beside me in utter despair.

His funeral was filled with friends and relatives, many of whom sympathized deeply with his former fiancée, Leesa. There was an unspoken fear among some of us that she might blame herself for his decision to end his life. The reasons behind his choice were never clear. On the morning of his death, Karen James called our house to inquire if I had returned from Adelaide. She mentioned he had sounded cheerful. As far as I know, Karen was the last person to ever speak to him—August 20, 1991.

The funeral sermon was unusually brief. The crowded corridors were filled with hundreds of mourners standing silently, occupying every available space. Beside me, my sister sat with her husband, Dave, consoling her. My parents sat motionless, gazing with hollow sorrow at the wooden casket adorned with flowers. Inside lay the lifeless body that had once been their son, my brother, my rock.

Regrettably, there was no opportunity for anyone to speak about my brother's life. No one shared stories of his admirable character, selfless acts of kindness, passion for cars, or unwavering love for Johnnie Walker.

I felt a desperate urge to say something. I wanted those present to know about the bond we shared and the memories we made during my childhood when he was my protective 'big brother.' He stood by me throughout my primary school years, reassuring me whenever I needed him. I admired his charisma with the ladies, which occasionally garnered attention because I was his younger brother. I distinctly recall feeling lost and alone when he moved on to secondary school without me.

My family struggled visibly throughout the service, but it was my sister who bore the weight of grief most openly. She had always been Colin's closest companion. I wanted to comfort her, to do something meaningful, but I felt lost in knowing what would be right.

That year, I strained my relationships with my siblings, mainly as I slowly began to 'come out' as gay. The process sometimes created tension between us, making an already difficult period even more challenging. Each step I took towards living my truth seemed to widen the gap between us, and the sense of alienation weighed heavily on my heart. Colin's death, however, brought us back together with a stark reminder of the importance of family and the fleeting nature of time. We became closer than we had been in years, which I believe brought some solace to our grieving parents.

Colin was laid to rest beside his younger sister, Lisa. Over three hundred messages in his memorial book echoed a common sentiment:

> *You left us so suddenly. We don't know why.*

He had been unwavering in following through with whatever had driven him to make this irreversible decision. We later discovered that his initial attempt had been unsuccessful, though the specifics remained undisclosed. When my mother returned home, hearing the faint hum of an engine and noticing the closed garage door, she rushed in and faced her worst fears.

Colin, I may not have had the chance to express the words I wanted to say at your funeral, but I will tell them now. You have always been, and will always be, my big brother. I love you deeply and miss you terribly. I hope the pain that led you to this choice has been lifted from your soul, allowing you to find peace and light in your journey.

10

DARK HORSE FROM DOWN UNDER

Australia hadn't hosted the World Championships since 1975, and the championships in Sydney were mere weeks after Colin's funeral. Finding the discipline to put in the necessary hours of preparation for the competition was agonizing. There were moments when I doubted my ability to cope, but somehow, I summoned the inner strength to continue. My parents and friends reassured me that Colin wouldn't want my career to suffer because of my grief.

We all understood the importance of maintaining my focus and determination to defend the silver medal ranking I had achieved in 1990. However, my training sessions didn't reflect that determination. I often stood aimlessly in the middle of the rink, lost in thought while the music played. I remember storming off the rink, ripping off my skates, and hurling one across the foyer, where it hit the wall. Then, I ran out to the car park, screaming at the top of my lungs. It didn't accomplish much, but I felt a little better afterward.

Did I miss an opportunity that could have prevented this overwhelming sense of loss? I had to push aside those thoughts, focus, and move forward. I needed to win another medal—this time for Colin.

In the lead-up to this championship, I rarely felt supported in my preparation. Although the Federation hoped for another medal, they offered no mental, physical, or financial assistance. While it wasn't 'expected,' it would have been helpful. One person who stood by me was an unlikely ally: my competitor and long-time friend, Lucas McKane.

In the weeks following Colin's death, Lucas visited our family home several times weekly. He would sit in my room, talking about nothing in particular, just being there and making me feel valued. We had known each other travelled to worlds together many times, but our friendship was mainly confined to the rink or occasional social stuff with other skaters. His support during that time meant more to me than he could ever know. In a small way, he filled the void left by Colin and provided much of the inner strength I needed in the lead-up to Sydney.

Disney World, FL 1988 - Jayson & Lucas

There were moments when many around me feared I might succumb to the pressure, but as the short program approached, I felt a hint of nerves creeping in. Despite the hype from official training sessions, which painted me as a strong contender, I didn't personally feel the part. During the figure section of the competition, constant uncertainty and doubt swirled in my mind. Although, I managed a decent result in the top ten. This meant that with a strong performance in the free skating, I had a chance at a medal in the combined event if nothing else.

There was a last-minute decision to ease the pressure of my new short program, which led to varying the difficulty and placement of the first three elements. I was okay with this until it counted. Once I got onto the floor and felt my legs surrender beneath me, I knew this wouldn't be a good skate. Stepping into that first jump, the double axel, I knew something was wrong. It didn't feel like any other double axel attempt I'd made. Milliseconds later, I was sprawled sideways on the floor in shock and panic. Was the triple-lutz combination next as initially planned, or the triple flip down the other end? I was lost for a few seconds, and before I could think clearly, I crashed into the floor again on the triple flip right in front of Charmaine. Our eyes connected, and I stared at her desperately, wanting this to end.

> *It's hard to imagine the pressure Jayson must have been under that year to perform, especially with everything that had happened—his brother passing away and the expectation from Australia for a medal-winning performance. I can't imagine how it must have felt to step out on that floor with all that weight on his shoulders. I can't even begin to imagine what that must have been like...*
> TAMMY BRYANT

As they say, things come in threes, and yes, I was down once more on the final jump element in the replacement combination. Everything that could go wrong did. I felt profound disappointment in myself and for Charmaine, helpless on the sideline, and especially for my mom, who I knew would be in tears in the stands, shaking while she wrote down the scores. It must have been tough for her to witness such a dismal performance, helpless on the sidelines. However, the program's failure wasn't the worst part. I could hear snide remarks being made deliberately within my earshot, something that is commonly known as 'tall poppy syndrome' in Australia. A small group of skaters from within my own country were happy to see me fail and unashamed to show it. Their insecurities and ignorance of what had just happened in my life allowed them to ridicule someone who grieved.

> *Jayson hadn't performed well in the short program and afterward, he sat with me for hours before preparing for his long program. We didn't say much; it was as if we didn't need to. It was one of the toughest years of his skating career, and while I couldn't help him achieve his peak performance, it was crucial for him to know how much support and love he had...* JODIE JOHNSON (GARUFO)

Mentally, I wasn't in a state to continue the competition. It felt like all my preparation for the event had vanished into thin air. My thoughts were muddled, and the focus I once had disappeared. To my surprise, my entire family showed up the next day to support me in the long program. I knew they just wanted to support me, and it was equally hard for them to watch, but their presence added to the pressure. Skating among the bottom group for the final event left me feeling defeated before I even began. But it wasn't over yet.

Despite ranking 22nd after the short program, I managed to climb to 9th place after the long program, fueled by a final burst of determination. It wasn't the medal-winning victory I had dreamt of, but it was a determined performance with Charmaine by my side. It was a bittersweet victory, as I found myself just behind my teammate Adrian Lomman, who had beaten me for the first time with an incredible performance, placing 8th.

Additionally, I finished fourth in the combined figures and free skating event. It was hard to accept this outcome, especially after being ranked second in the world the previous year, but it fueled my determination to come back stronger the following year. I had invested too much in this journey to let it end there.

> *When you have a bad performance, there are two things that can happen: you can let it defeat you, which is what many people in Australia did when they wrote Jayson off after his performance in 1991, or you can use it to propel yourself forward, striving for bigger and better things, igniting your passion and driving you to improve and make things better...* TAMMY BRYANT

Death continued to linger over me like a haunting whisper, spreading its sadistic pleasure. The skating community mourned the loss of Jodie Hutchinson, one of Australia's most beloved athletes, on February 22nd, 1992. Jodie was a loving and caring daughter and the twin sister of my close friend Jonelle. That afternoon, Jodie left the rink due to a severe headache and tragically collapsed and passed away shortly afterward at home. The news was devastating for her family, and like everyone else, I was deeply shocked and saddened by her sudden departure. Jodie's infectious smile had endeared her to all who knew her. Alongside Jonelle, she had been among Australia's most popular and successful twins in skating. In a show of respect, a minute of silence was observed at a local competition in Queensland the next day. Around four hundred mourners gathered on February 28th for her funeral, bidding a final farewell to this remarkable young woman.

Jodie Hutchinson, Jayson and Tammy

" Jodie and I were fortunate enough to discover artistic rollerskating at age seven at our local rink, West Coast, in Craigie, WA.

We spent many years training, competing, and traveling together, forming lifelong friendships that continue to this day. When we lost Jodie, the support from our skating community was unwavering. Everyone who knew her loved her, and it was comforting to be surrounded by others from our beloved sport during such a difficult time. I cherish every single day of the 18 years we had together...
JONELLE HUTCHINSON (McKANE)

As I plunged back into training, I decided to venture out alone. My visits to Adelaide ceased, and sadly, over the following months, I gradually lost touch with Charmaine. It wasn't Charmaine's fault—we had worked incredibly well together over the past year. But other aspects of my life were taking a toll. Deep down, I felt the need to be independent, to go it alone and be responsible for any mistakes I might make in the future. I still hadn't come to terms with the loss of my brother, the failure in Sydney still haunted me, and my hidden sexuality remained the heaviest burden I longed to lift.

To add fuel to the fire, I began dabbling in ice skating. For a while, I felt I had achieved my goals in roller skating and lacked the drive to go further. Ice skating proved to be a new challenge. I started working with Robyn Burley at the Olympic Ice Centre, and before long, the techniques I was learning on the ice began interfering with my roller skating jumps. While many skaters managed to balance both, I struggled. Eventually, I had to choose between the two. Roller skating won.

It was then that I chose to take on my own students. Fred and Mary Slade approached me after the World Meet, asking if I would coach their eight-year-old daughter, Kristen, who was fiercely dedicated to the sport. We immediately clicked, and our connection quickly yielded positive results. Their commitment to Kristen's sport was unyielding. They drove from Geelong to Melbourne five to six times per week and had been doing morning sessions before school. When I told Mary Kristen's lessons would be at 6:45, she gasped, "Oh, that's late, we're used to 5:30." It was only shortly after that

I realized she meant AM, not PM! There was no way I was doing those early starters. That's one thing roller skating has over ice skating—not so many cold, early mornings!

Balancing coaching and my training wasn't easy, so I initially only took on two students: Kristen and Kathy Mason. It was quite a contrast—coaching an eight-year-old alongside an eighteen-year-old—but it gave me a steep learning curve from which I learned from many mistakes. The ultimate reward, however, came from witnessing young skaters transform from beginners to National Champions. Now I understand the bittersweet feeling a coach experiences when their students move on because students often become like your own children. As a teacher and coach, nurturing and guiding their development until they blossom fully is incredibly fulfilling. Few professions can match the profound rewards of this journey.

> *I remember hearing that Jayson wanted to take on skaters, and he had always been someone I idolized. I spent countless hours watching videos of him skate. So, when he agreed to take me on, I was over the moon. Starting at Noble Park with a new way of training, everything quickly began to click, and I felt like I was finally on the right path...*
> *KATHY MASON (CRETTENDEN)*

Kristen excelled at the subsequent national meet, securing two gold medals amid strong fields in the figures and free skating events. I performed an exhibition at the opening of the nationals, marking the start of my gradual shift towards a new phase—PERFORMANCE.

Eager to introduce something distinctive to the arena, I performed to the music from Swan Lake for this occasion. Clad in a sleek, black Lycra head-to-toe bodysuit adorned with shimmering swirls of color, complemented by full face makeup to capture the essence of the character, I reveled in every moment of the routine, hoping it translated to the audience. Initially, the skin suit was plain black. But Liz and Jillian transformed it in our hotel room just hours before the performance. While I wore the suit in the kitchenette, they painted intricate swirls and glued glitter onto it, ensuring a perfect finish.

Certain pieces of music have a profound emotional connection with audiences, and I believe Swan Lake is one of those pieces. While skating this routine, I experienced one of those rare moments of complete immersion in the music, where all other thoughts and distractions faded.

I was pleased with my competitive performance that year, too. Adrian Lomman and I were picking up where we left off in Sydney. This time, I found my feet again and retained my title. It was a definite improvement from my efforts in Sydney, which gave me confidence that I had a real shot at the upcoming world championships in the US. It was also my first national title, where I competed without a coach by my side, there to support me. This was all part of the 'plan,' but it didn't feel significant enough to sustain international success. I knew I needed to change it up a notch. That's when I boldly decided to pack up and train with a coach in America. I spent nearly two months there that year, dedicated to getting into peak condition for the major event in Florida.

So, USA it was. While training with Petra Dayney in Ohio, a revered former World Champion known for her tough yet respected coaching style, I knew it would be a tough seven weeks of hard work. I had known Petra for years and worked alongside her at a seminar in Sydney for five days at the Campbelltown rink. It was a grueling week in excruciating heat during the Summer. We would rush back to the hotel, conveniently located next door to the rink, and Petra would plunge her feet into buckets of iced water with a sigh of relief, and I would dive into the pool and splash about with other skaters cooling off.

Petra's training regimen was exceptionally demanding, surpassing my previous experiences. Although figures were not my favorite, I understood their critical role in enhancing my overall skating skills and rankings, so I committed to at least two hours of practice daily to improve them alongside her daughter, April. Mark Lind used to rave about April when I was younger, as he'd been to the U.S. Nationals one year prior and seen her compete. So I was always keen to see this young girl with all the 'double loops' who was only an eight—or nine-year-old at the time. Now, I was training with her daily and living at her house, and she was learning to drive!

> *In the fall of 1992, Jayson trained with me in the USA, and it was more than just roller skating. He was also teaching me how to drive. Yes, in Australia, they drive on the other side of the road, but no, that's not why I failed my driving test twice! I vividly recall one evening after skating practice when Jay, Tracy Black, and I headed over to the empty parking lot of a local convenience store. We waited for it to close and clear out so we could practice without risking hitting any vehicles.*
>
> *I had failed my first driving test due to my inability to parallel park the "land yacht" my parents drove. So, the guys flipped over shopping carts to recreate the parallel parking scenario. After a couple of hours and a ton of patience on their part, I was finally able to parallel park successfully! I owe my stellar parking skills to Jayson and Tracy, and I will forever think of that evening whenever I have to park the car. Thanks, Jayson, for not only the skating memories but also the life skills I continue to use daily!...* APRIL DAYNEY (JACOBSON)

Within a week of training in Ohio, everything started to fall into place. My nerves had settled, and I found myself embracing a routine with confidence and a clear understanding of the mission. Petra was all business, and there was no room for messing around. Often, I'd end a session flat on my back on the carpet, with a wet towel over my face and my feet in a bucket of water. It was agony and ecstasy at the same time.

Petra had watched me perform my short program several times. One day, she stood up from the sidelines and said,

> *You need a new short program. I don't like this one.*

Initially, I planned to skate to music from 'Hook' for my two-minute program in Tampa, Florida; Petra believed a classical piece would offer greater artistic appeal, as Hook differed too little from my long program. I vividly recall sitting in Petra's lounge, exploring her record collection and listening to beloved ballets and concertos. Petra chose 'Gypsy Dance,' a traditional gypsy melody that captivated me instantly. What fascinated me, even more, was how she edited the music using a device I had never seen before, a reel-to-reel tape deck resembling a film projector. Watching her splice the reels together to create the perfect cuts in the music amazed me.

The next day, we began working on the new program, and surprisingly, we completed it quickly during the session. While we retained much of the program's original structure, we made significant changes to the choreography and footwork, which proved beneficial in showcasing my improved strength and consistency in Tampa. However, one requirement was creating a new costume to complement the performance.

Petra was pleasantly surprised when she discovered I could create the costume using her sewing machine. Considering the music's period theme, I chose a classic design using a luxurious crème silk fabric we found at one of Petra's preferred stores. I carefully sewed single pleats along the sleeves and added delicate chiffon cuffs adorned with gold braid. It was my first attempt at such detailed craftsmanship, and predictably, it became my favorite costume, one I cherished for years. Unlike many others I had hastily sewn and discarded, this costume departed from my previous habits, driven solely by the convenience of my sewing skills.

When my training stint in Ohio concluded, having worked tirelessly alongside April each day, I felt as steady as a rock on wheels. I had never felt so consistent before, nor had I executed so many programs in succession. Petra's approach was rigorous; she would insist on a complete long program within minutes of stepping onto the rink each session—considered a warm-up! And if you weren't ready, bad luck! The music would come on, and you'd have to get moving. It was the most effective method of honing my skills for a world championship that I had ever encountered. I knew it deep down—I was fully prepared to take on the competition.

On the initial day in Tampa, I re-joined my fellow Australian team members for our first off-site training session. It was beautiful to see Kirsten and Tammy again. I missed traveling to Adelaide and seeing Tammy often, and I only had the chance to catch up with Kirsten once or twice a year. A peculiar mix of calm and adrenaline coursed through me, aware that my performance would catch everyone off guard. And indeed, it did. It was one of the most exceptional training sessions I had ever experienced. As I executed my programs, the rink cleared, and all eyes focused on me, including those of team manager Harry Bracegirdle, who appeared somewhat gratified to see me regain my footing after our shared disappointment at the previous year's meet. His support and encouragement were greatly appreciated at the time. We didn't share many words, but there was a genuine understanding between us.

Petra could not attend the short program competition due to severe back issues that almost kept her from traveling. Peggy Yambor, the rink owner from Ohio, stood by me rink-side, along with the enthusiastic assistant team manager, Carol Jessop. Despite drawing an early position, third in the skating order, my nerves were surprisingly absent this time. However, a small mistake on my double axel proved costly, allowing other competitors to surpass me. I was frustrated with myself, knowing April would slap me for 'popping' it, something she had seen me execute flawlessly in training countless times. Nevertheless, I secured sixth place in the short program, securing a spot in the top group for the long program on the final night.

Approaching the long program, the last phase was the official training for the top group of skaters, the most anticipated session of the week. Everybody wants to watch it because they know it's a "one for all" playoff. The auditorium surged with adrenaline from the floor to the sideline. It was an incredibly intensive session, often producing better performances than in the final competition. My run of the long program was without fault, leaving a few other coaches and skaters looking somewhat nervous. I was used to doing this program within minutes of warming up. Here, I'd had more than twenty-five, given I had an excellent draw for the long program - second to last, with only Patrick Venerucci of Italy to follow.

I noticed Charmaine watching the session from the stands with Tammy. It saddened me that we were not together, and it brought to mind something she had once said to me.

> *I respect a winner who loses and comes back again.*

At that moment, it felt more real than ever. On the night of the competition, my nerves were in check, and Petra was able to attend. I felt like I owed her a great skate after all the work she had put in over the past weeks. As I skated late in the group, I had ample time to observe the other competitors. I noticed very few faults among them, and I couldn't deny feeling nervous at this point. However, I took solace in knowing I had prepared for this meet meticulously, leaving no stone unturned. There was a real chance to improve from sixth place in the standings, and there was no way I was going to miss that double axel again! The thought of disappointing my mom by missing out on a medal motivated me even more—I was determined to give it everything.

Petra exuded an elegant calmness despite her back pain. Seated front and center next to the entry gate, she appeared to have done it all a thousand times before and relished every moment. And, just as she predicted, my performance that night was one of the best of my career. Every element was executed effortlessly, like in training, except for one jump—the triple salchow, which I rotated as a double. If I had missed that jump in training back in Ohio, Petra would have made me repeat the program, so I got off lightly that night. The judges' scores, however, were mixed but were good enough to propel me from sixth place in the short program to the world No. 2 position.

When the confirmation came through that I had won my second world silver medal, it took everyone by surprise, even me, to an extent. But it proved one thing—I was back! I ran straight to the telephone to let my parents know I had kicked some serious butt. The US television commentary team summed it up best: "Jayson Sutcliffe is a dark horse from down under."

After my first world medal-winning performance, I wondered,

> *Can I do this again?*

Now I had my answer, and the best was yet to come.

The championship's closing banquet was held at the Busch Gardens theme park. It was a private function with about 500 people in attendance, and awards were presented to all the medal winners. Each successful athlete was called to the platform to receive a prestigious triangular marble block engraved with our names and rankings. I hadn't received anything like this before; it reminded me of an MTV Award.

Following a short stint in L.A. with Kirsten Murphy and her family, I returned home and visited Colin's grave. I hadn't gone there often, maybe twice since he died. It was too hard for me to go and "talk to him." After his death, I also felt terrible about performing poorly at the championships. In some dark corner of my mind, I wondered if Colin thought I blamed him. That certainly wasn't the case, and now, with good news to share, I could finally explain that to him.

Colin had always wanted me to "kick ass." As I lay on the damp grass, I felt his warmth. I enjoyed the silence until I decided to tell him the news.

And I added, "I did it for you."

'You have to DREAM it!'

11

HOME AWAY FROM HOME

In early January 1993, Italian coach Alvia Vitta and former world champion Sandro Guerra were invited to Australia to conduct a series of seminars nationwide. I was asked to join the trip as a guest coach, which began in Perth, the first of four states we would visit. Sandro and I both skated an exhibition at the Morley Rollerdrome to conclude our first seminar, and it was something we weren't to repeat in the following stages. So, that was a special gift for the WA skaters, seeing Sandro perform live and for the last time in our country as he retired after the world championships in 1992.

One of the highlights during these camps was the choreography sessions led by Sandro, with me as his sidekick. He asked if I had a 'good song' we could perform to, and I naturally suggested a selection from Kylie's latest album, Let's Get to It. Sandro loved the track 'Right Here, Right Now,' and we chose it for the upbeat class and a more subdued piece for the classical side of things.

The kids loved the upbeat section, filling the room with giggles and cries of nerves as they performed in a single line. This hands-on experience was why international seminars benefited our skaters so greatly. We ran them annually to give skaters exposure that wasn't easily accessed through a mobile device or a paid app with instant tuition. This was hands-on, once-in-a-lifetime (or year) stuff you could sink your teeth into, and they loved it.

Sandro and Jayson with one of the three groups in Melbourne, 1993

This tour marked the last time we would see former skater and Oceania champion Melissa George on skates before her rise to Hollywood fame. I had known Melissa for several years and was amazed to learn she was about to start work on the popular Australian television drama series, "Home & Away." It was like a fairy tale. We would write letters to each other and talk about our favorite songs and any 'gossip' in skating. Aside from competing in artistic roller skating, she was very young and had only been doing some part-time modeling. Her big break came when her agent convinced her to audition for a role in the hit series. Trying to explain to Sandro the enormity of the opportunity presented to her was difficult. Eventually, he understood Melissa was on the verge of celebrity status and stardom.

> *The last time I ever skated was the day before I went on to star in Home & Away. Jayson was in Perth for the seminar with the Italians and witnessed the best skating day I had ever had. I was doing jump combinations that even I was shocked at.*
>
> *In the days following that memorable moment, I hung up my skates and took off to Sydney to start my new life, but no matter where I go, I will always consider Jayson my mentor...*
> *MELISSA GEORGE*

Back in Melbourne, my role as a skating coach was progressing well. My youngest students, Kristen Slade and Melissa Ambrose, showed significant progress. I also started teaching in Geelong, 45 minutes outside of Melbourne. I had a handful of skaters there who appreciated my twice-weekly trips. Kristen had already won two National titles, the first of more than many we would win together over our decade-plus-long working relationship.

In 1993, another turning point came into my life. I was awarded 'Sports Star of The Year' by the local Community Credit Union and Leader Newspaper, thanks to my current World No. 2 ranking. I had previously won the 'Sports Star of The Future' award in 1991, making me the first athlete to win both. This achievement was even sweeter because several athletes in my district had achieved excellent results in high-profile sports and events. It was one of the few and highly treasured moments when roller sports received well-deserved recognition.

Winning this award suddenly gave roller sports credibility outside the roller-skating fraternity, making it even more significant. As an athlete, all the effort and commitment I had put in were finally being acknowledged, just as they would be in any other sport. It wasn't like I had overnight celebrity status, but winning and being reported in the papers made people recognize me on the street. It was also a huge advantage when I applied for financial assistance to train overseas with new coaches. Slowly, I was climbing the ladder I had built for myself. Just how high could I climb? I kept asking.

The World Games that year marked my second participation in the four-yearly event, this time held in The Hague, a coastal area in the Netherlands teeming with tourists despite the bitterly cold weather. Our hotel was just up from the ocean's edge and within walking distance of the town. Bill Begg, our team manager, needed no introduction, though we had not had much contact since a training camp in Melbourne at Monash University in 1989. As the team's physical adviser, he was appalled by our condition, considering we were the best in Australia. His honesty served as a wake-up call for many of us. Bill Begg is to speed skating what the legendary Don Talbot is to Australian swimming. Bill has taken several countries, including Australia, Colombia, and New Zealand, from obscurity to being ranked No. 1 in the world.

I got to know Bill quite well during our time in The Hague. He was an inspiring character with many great stories about his life and times in our sport. I could sit for hours exchanging memories with him, but my main interest was how he motivated the teams he worked with to become No. 1 in the world. His methods seemed brutal, but they were necessary for success in speed skating.

One day, he asked me if I had ever dreamed of becoming a world champion. I had to be honest and admit that, although it was always what I had wanted, I had never actually dreamed about it. From that moment, the thought played on my mind for the entire day. It was my lifelong dream, yet I had never actually visualized it in my dreams.

Bill's words repeated tirelessly in my head:

> *"You have to dream it. You have to dream it."*

It was the last thought I had that night before going to sleep. The next day, I raced up to Bill in amazement.

"I did it," I told him. "I had the dream."

"Jayson," he said, shaking my hand. "Good on you, mate. The day will now come."

The truth of his words is now history, but I firmly believe it was because someone made me SEE I could do it that it finally happened. However, that day had yet to arrive.

On the second morning in The Hague, as suggested by Bill, I borrowed a pair of inline speed skates and went road training with the team. It was the first time I had worn inline skates, let alone a five-wheel pair of fiberglass-molded boots. Looking back at this, I realize it wasn't genius to do this; I could have easily twisted my ankle. The ride was long but exhilarating. There were several smooth, concreted paths along the beach, many with winding curves and hills extending onto the main pier. The speeds increased as we skated further along the tracks, not easing even when we ventured into busier areas. Team members dodged people like totem poles set on a slalom run. I could feel the chill biting into my face. My teeth felt so brittle I thought they might snap if I gritted them. I almost believed I was on a slalom path with snow beneath my feet and icicles forming on my chin.

I wasn't as well equipped as the others with winter clothing, though thankfully, Bill gave me gloves. Desley Hill, team member, and world speed champion led the pack. Foolishly, I joked with her about skating off the side of the pier. I shouldn't have. No sooner had I said those fateful words than I nearly crossed the edge. I had forgotten I didn't have rubber toe-stops on the front of these skates.

Sadly, the Games were disappointing in terms of spectators compared to the previous event, which had capacity crowds. The Hague had maybe two hundred spectators at the skating events. Sponsorship problems affected all the events. We were also disappointed with the venue's standard, which looked like it had been thrown together with leftover building materials. But we adapted and soldiered on. Upon arrival, we were shown to a pristine auditorium with raised seating. It looked perfect. "Wow, is this the stadium?" I asked. As she led us through a small entrance to the side, the guide replied, "No. You're out here." The look on all our faces said it all. It was a big shed with a wooden floor and some temporary seating—dampening our enthusiasm.

I skated the short program I used at the World Meet in 1992, which Petra choreographed for me. Annoyingly, I suffered the same problem in Tampa, missing that double axel 'again' in the short, leaving me in fourth position behind Samo Kokorovec, Jamie Smith, and Heath Medeiros. In the back of my mind, there was only one thought: to surpass the skater from the UK and claim the bronze medal. That was my goal for the day ahead.

During the training session for the long program, I realized that Samo, from Northern Italy, with his blonde hair and good looks, had the same music and arrangement as I did. We were both using selections from Vivaldi's "Four Seasons." It was my turn to skate next, but I couldn't see how having two skaters in the top four performing to the same music would work with the judges. So, in a last-minute decision, I opted to change my music. I had planned to use the new long program I had performed at our national championships only weeks before in Perth. Instead, I raced over to my skate bag and shuffled through it, hoping I still had a copy of my music from the previous year. I did! A badly worn-out cassette, labeled with a pen marker, 'Jayson - 92 Long.' So, it seemed I would give Edward Scissorhands another run, having already performed it for two years. It was a good choice; I skated my Aussie butt off for four minutes that afternoon, earning my highest mark at an international event for my long program: 9.9 (now scored out of ten) from the French judge (thank you!), pushing me into second position. Medeiros took the gold and Kokorovec the bronze.

Weeks later, after the event and returning to Australia, Kirsten Murphy and I decided to travel together to Italy to train at the 'Jolly Club' in Trieste with Mario and Alvia Vitta, home of the legend Sandro Guerra, ahead of the world championships in France. I couldn't afford to return to the States to work with Petra and travel to Europe before the meet, so choosing a cost-effective option in Europe made sense. However, Kirsten struggled with being away from home, and her time in Italy proved challenging. I hoped she would adjust, but with each passing day, she seemed more unsettled. Traveling is always nice, but sometimes, there's nothing like being home when you're far from it.

In the early hours of one morning, I received the dreaded call. It was her sister, Kylie, from Australia, with devastating news. Never did I imagine I would personally know of one suicide in my life, let alone two. This dark path had haunted me in the recent past. Hearing the heartbreaking news brought back a flood of painful memories and images I thought I had left behind long ago.

Kylie couldn't bring herself to deliver the news directly. She pleaded with me to do it for her. My heart sank. How do you tell someone that their loved one has taken their own life? Fate intervened; Kirsten stood at the door as I took the call. Her face crumbled, and she collapsed into my arms, overcome with inconsolable grief. Mario and Alvia, waking to the commotion, were stunned into silence and disbelief as I explained the situation.

Kirsten was devastated, as anybody would be in this situation. Within days, her mother and long-time friend, Janice, arrived. It was an awkward situation for them both, as so many unanswered questions always seem to shroud suicides. But Kirsten was strong. A week later, I managed to get her back on skates and do some training. Her mother encouraged her, seeming to know intuitively what I had learned from experience – staying occupied was the best way to get on with life. The world championships were less than two weeks away, and Kirsten was still eager to compete. In retrospect, if I had to decide again about competing in 1991 after Colin's death, I wouldn't have. But this time, Jan and I believed it was the right choice for Kirsten. I hope we made the right decision. It wasn't an option for us at this late stage to return to Australia for the funeral. So, we remained in Italy, offering as much support as we could, in my case, sympathizing with her pain on a very personal level.

1993 Worlds - Kirsten, Jayson & Sandro Guerra

France was a country I had heard so much about and seen in countless movies and TV shows. It was also the setting for one of my favorite Kylie video clips, "Finer Feelings," beautifully filmed around the Eiffel Tower. Naturally, my first thought upon returning was to visit the tower and take some photos, in black and white, of course. We traveled to Montpelier for a brief stop from Paris before heading to Bordeaux.

Everything had gone smoothly until then. Kirsten, Janice, and I stood at another luggage carousel, waiting for our bags. One by one, everyone collected their luggage—except me. Jan moaned and laughed, "Oh god, not again." She was right. I watched and waited, hoping my case would appear. Had it been left on the plane? No such luck! My luggage was off to another destination, with all my competition outfits inside. Skating outfits are personalized and custom-made, and I make all my own, so wearing anything else feels uncomfortable. You cannot pick them up at a store unless you have no choice!

I started to panic and filed a report with lost and found. Airport staff assured me they would contact me as soon as the bags were found, advising me to continue my way for now. I was furious at how calm they were about the incident. My life depended on these competitions; the costumes were just as important as the performance (maybe that was a little Montpelier, but they were essential!). I hoped they would find my luggage within the next two days before the competition began.

Three days into our stay in Bordeaux, there was still no sign of my luggage. I shared a room with Michael Rose, who was kind enough to let me use some of his gear. To the airline's credit, they compensated me daily until my bags arrived. The silver lining was that I had a great time shopping in French stores, but it didn't solve the problem.

The solution came from Carmen, an aptly named Spanish store owner and skating fan. Her tailor-made costumes were on sale at the championships and fit perfectly! After much deliberation, I opted for a simple black top that I wore for both competitions, despite many people's annoyance.

Thankfully, when Sandro Guerra arrived in Bordeaux, he brought a small bag of clothes I had left at the rink in Trieste. I was overjoyed to see that it included a pair of my skating pants. Nothing fit as well as the pants I made for myself, and I was incredibly grateful to have them back.

The competition in France was intense, much stronger than in 1992. Italian newcomer Mauro Mazzoni looked formidable, and Samo Kokorovec had significantly improved since the World Games in The Hague a few weeks earlier, consistently nailing a nice triple loop. While competing internationally for the first time, Mauro included some challenging elements in his programs, like a triple Lutz combination, which was rare back then. Eric Anderson, Heath Medeiros, and Patrick Venerucci were all top contenders, effortlessly completing their triple jumps and combinations, ultimately putting the pressure on them.

Medeiros never cracked under pressure. He was a ball of dynamite that exploded post-1991. He had been on the world scene since his debut in Roccarasso in 1989. His first three world meets saw him ranking outside the top four positions, but it happened at the world meet in 1992—he became the world champion.

Heath's fire was still burning red hot. He wanted to retain his title just as much as Eric, and I was determined to take it from him. The short program competition was incredibly close for the top five skaters. Heath led with a stellar performance, earning scores in the high nines, and I received my first No.1 ordinal from one of the judges, the American. I'm sure that would have pissed off Heath and Eric, given they are from the US, but hey, I'll take it. While the overall standings didn't change much, seeing that number one ordinal on the official results sheet felt fantastic. Knowing that one judge had placed me first put a massive smile on my face and boosted my spirit for the long program.

I was ranked third for the short program, though the ordinals varied dramatically, narrowing the gap between second, third, fourth, and fifth. The competition ahead was tough, and we all knew we had to skate our best to stay in the top three.

I felt confident about holding my position on the night of the final. The unofficial training that morning and my event warm-up had gone exceptionally well. However, luck wasn't on my side when the draw placed me first to skate in the final group. Skaters always pray they don't draw first because the judge's scores have to be averaged out, but it is the luck of the draw. As I prepared to take the floor, nervous with anticipation, Patrick Venerucci from Italy attempted one last jump while skating toward the exit—an impressive one! But believe this or not, his toe stop went right through the sprung wooden floor.

It was incredible; I had never seen anything like it, and neither had anyone else watching. Patrick was fortunate; he could have seriously injured his ankle, but thankfully, the only damage was to the floor.

The incident threw the event organizers into a panic. It was clear from their faces that no one knew how to repair the damaged section of the floor, leading to a significant delay as frantic discussions occurred. The moment was completely disrupted. I had been fired up and full of adrenaline, ready to compete, but now there was a gaping hole in the floor, messing with my peak readiness.

The floor staff announced a delay of up to fifteen minutes. I mindlessly kept training the entire time, pushing myself harder than necessary. I felt good on the floor and didn't want to sit and cool off. However, the longer I trained, the more tense I became, so I figured it wouldn't hurt to keep going. Big mistake!

Mario Vitta waved to me from the sideline. "Jayson," he whispered loudly, "It's okay. Stop. Enough. You have done too much. Stop now." His advice was on point. At that moment, I realized I was feeling fatigued. Then, to my surprise, they announced the program was ready to commence. My name was called, catching me completely unaware. Suddenly, it was all action—go, go, go.

My planned opening move was a triple Lutz jump toward the bottom corner of the floor, precisely where Patrick had performed his. I had easily completed five or six of them during the warm-up, so I felt confident about nailing it. However, just as I was lining up for the jump and about to take off, a loud noise erupted from the speaker, breaking my concentration and preventing me from completing the rotation mid-air. I 'popped' it, reminiscent of those double axels in previous years. The music continued uninterrupted, but the noise threw me off. The speakers were placed in each corner of the floor, and it felt like I was jumping on top of them.

The remainder of my program lacked strength, although my triple flip was flawless, which was crucial. As the program neared its end, it was time for that dreaded double axel again, and fear, compounded by my mounting nerves, set in. I had a real phobia about this jump in the program, even though I had executed it brilliantly in the short program the day before. Falling on it in the long program was a stupid and costly mistake. It would be a close call between Samo, from Italy, and me for third place. He executed a spectacular triple-loop jump, and I thought I was out of the standings for sure. However, the scores disagreed with me. I narrowly took the bronze, edging out Kokorovec. My average efforts in the figure event also earned me bronze in the combined figures and free skating events, marking my first world medal for the combined event.

By the end of the championships, my luggage still hadn't arrived, and there was no word from the airline on whether it would reach Bordeaux before I departed. At the closing dinner banquet, I found myself without anything special to wear, so I wore the same jeans, t-shirt, and denim jacket I had worn casually throughout the week. The party was extravagant, in true French style, with a plush venue and an exquisite menu. To say my casual attire stood out would be an understatement, but I was comfortable, and it didn't stop me from enjoying myself.

The following day, our bus departed Bordeaux early. Many athletes looked worse for wear, having packed their luggage as an afterthought while nursing hangovers. As a seasoned competitor, I had wisely packed my essentials before the party, not forgetting I didn't have that much. I looked forward to returning to Paris to immerse myself in art and fashion. I also hoped to visit landmarks like Versailles, Notre Dame, and other historic sites.

My introduction to driving in the streets of Paris was beyond anything I could have imagined. Nothing in Australia had prepared me for this! The speed and intensity of the traffic were incredible. I lost a hubcap from the rear wheel on a sharp curb within just twenty minutes. Oh well.

I was sharing a hotel with Kirsten and Jan, and we had rented a car together. Neither of them dared to drive. Soon, I would reunite with Charmaine and the Bryant's, which was something I eagerly anticipated. We always had a lot of fun together, and this trip was to be no exception.

> *We had some really wild times, a lot of fun. I remember one year at worlds, we were playing pool at the hotel one night, just relaxing during downtime. Jayson hit the billiard ball so hard it flew off the table and rolled into the swimming pool. It was pitch black outside, but he decided to strip off his clothes, jump in, and retrieve the ball, no matter what.*
>
> *My mum happened to walk out at that moment, and Jayson jokingly asked, "Yvonne, wanna see the moon tonight? It's out!" (laughs) He then did this big somersault in the water, and out popped his bum— it was just the funniest thing...*
> TAMMY BRYANT

The moment I saw Charmaine, I knew we would reconnect. The distance in our once-close relationship took a significant step forward. Any lingering apprehension faded as we exchanged smiles. Passing glances brought back instant memories of our remarkable past together. I released a breath I hadn't realized I was holding, confident our bond would reignite and endure. And just like that, over coffee and croissants, it felt like we could have been sitting at Alfresco Café in North Adelaide, again, as we had done so many times before.

As our time in Paris ended, we parted with a heartfelt embrace. I missed hugging Charmaine and having her by my side when I competed. But, once again, we were united, looking forward to whatever the future held for us.

'I wanted to BLUR THAT LINE and test the limits that had been carved out by the HISTORY of skating.'

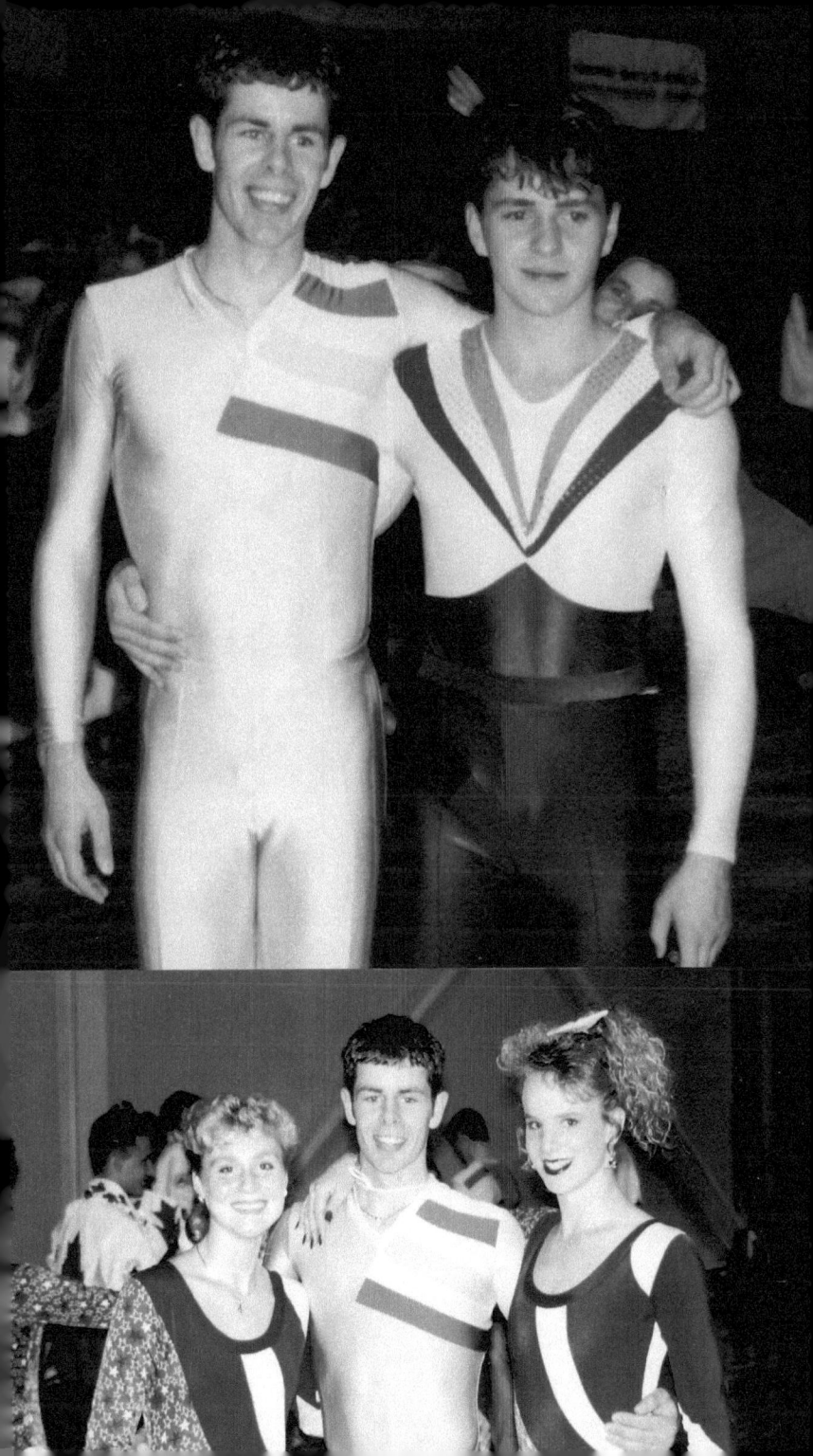

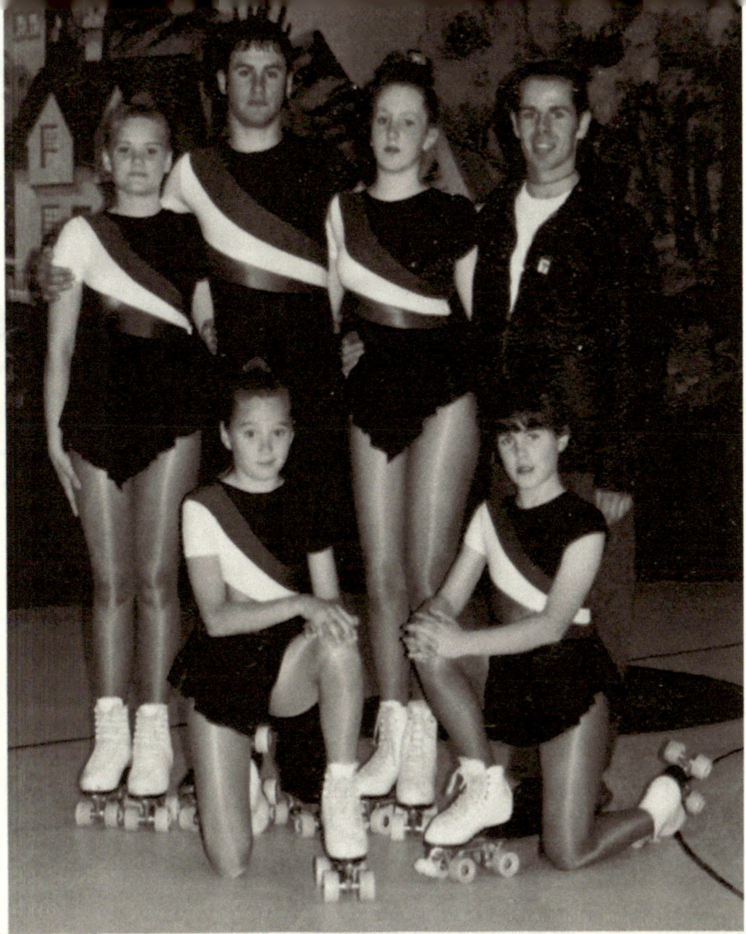

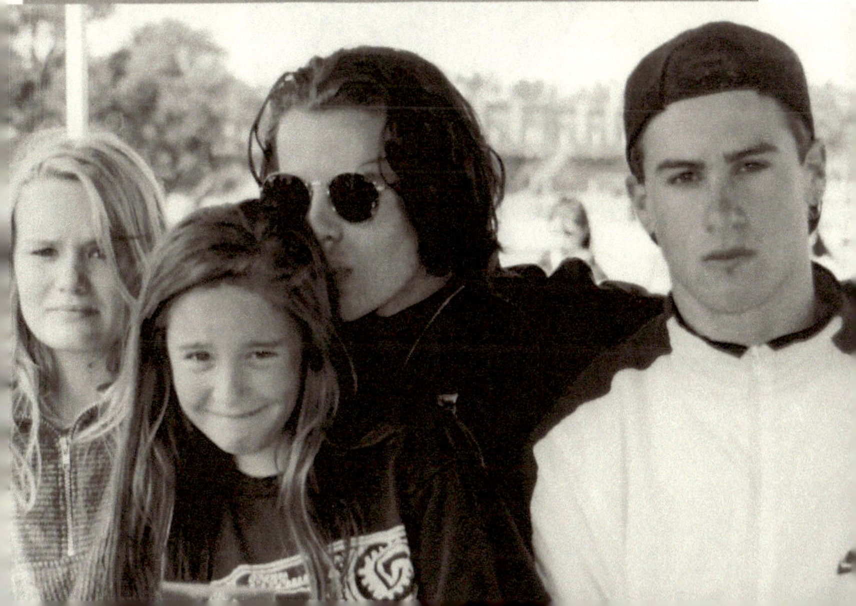

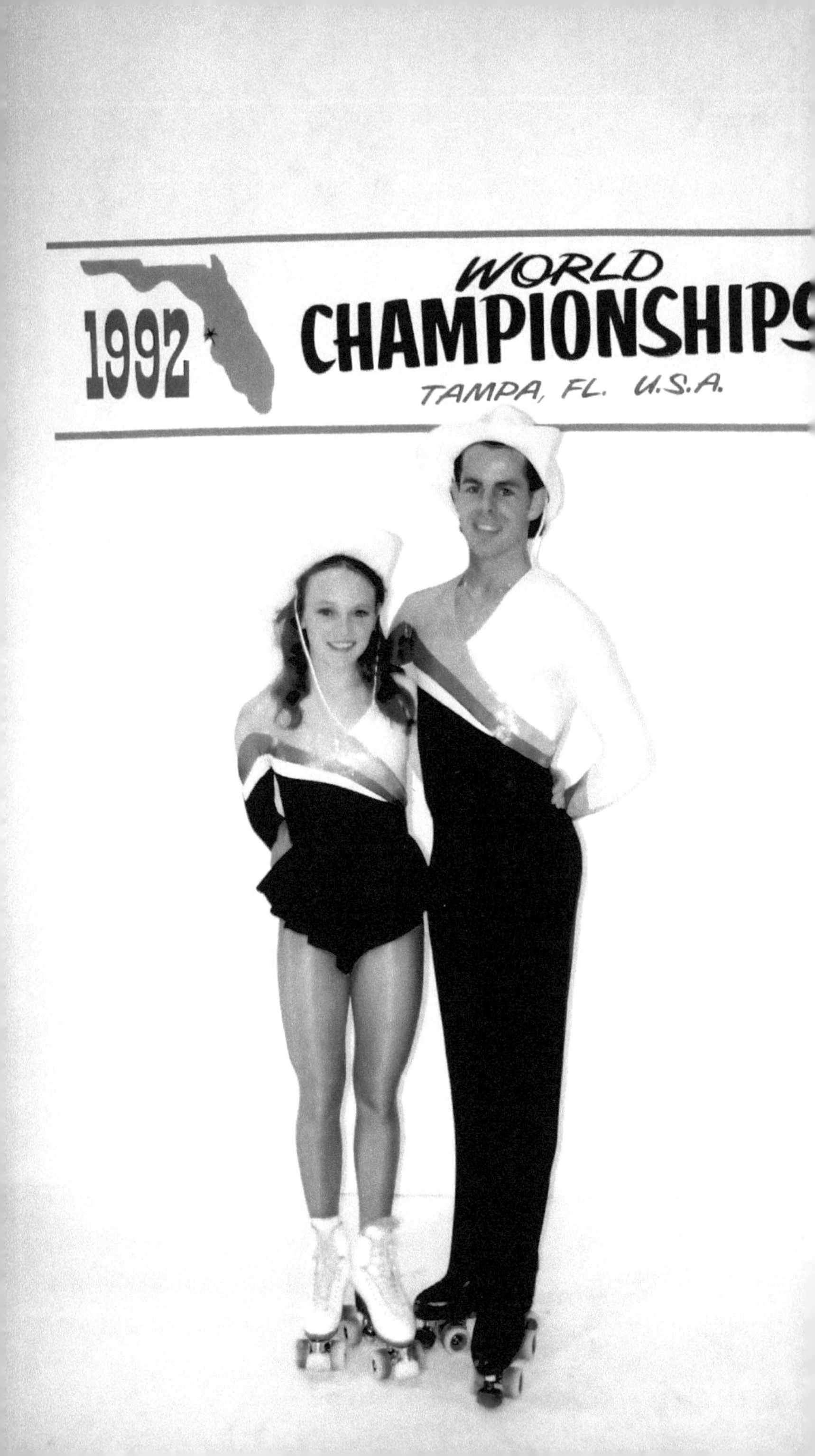
1992
WORLD
CHAMPIONSHIPS
TAMPA, FL. U.S.A.

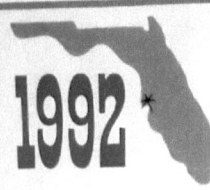

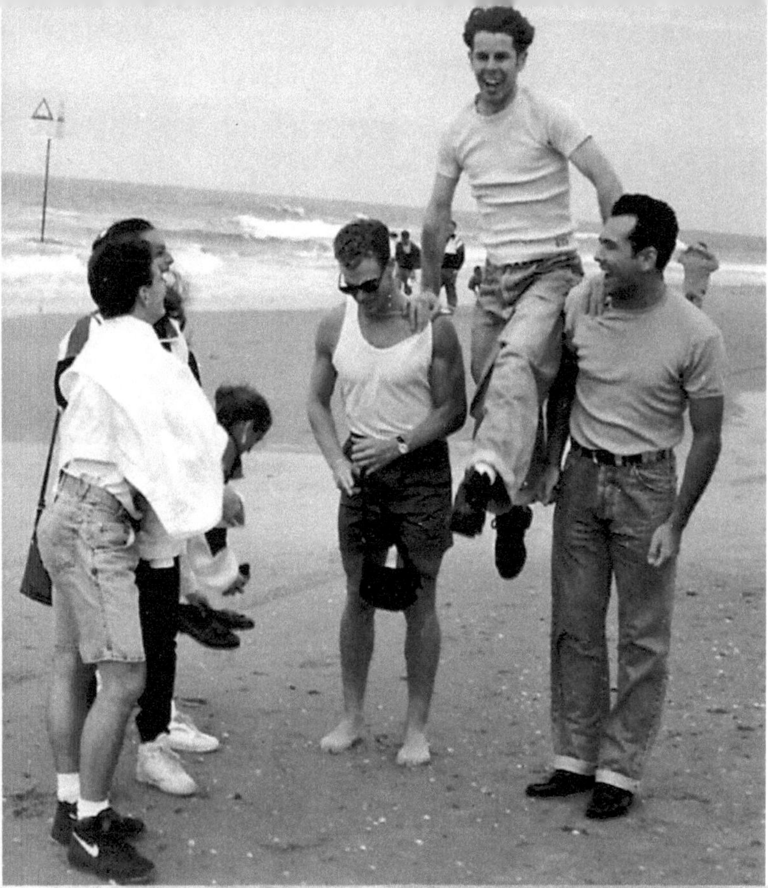

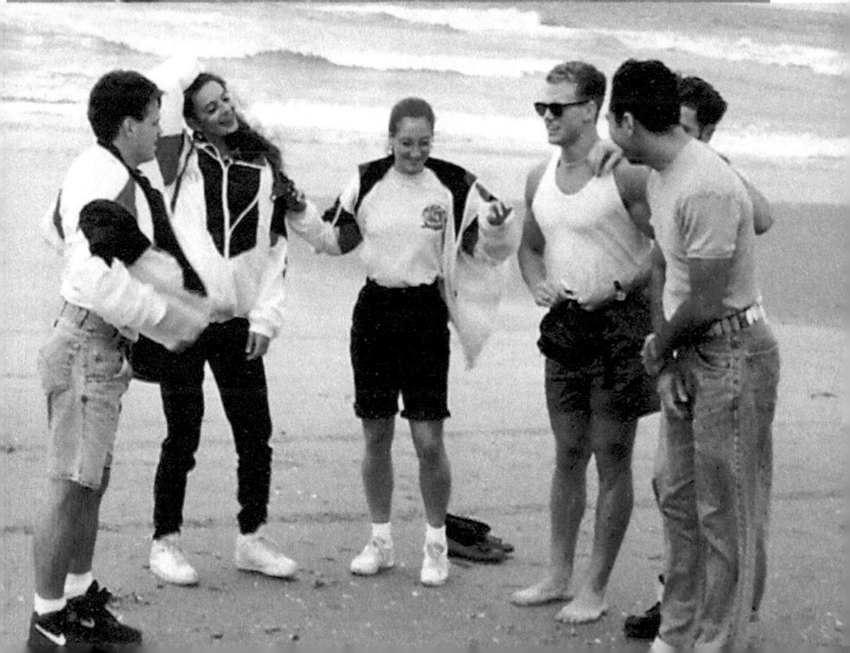

12

THE NEW APPROACH

In early 1994, I received an invitation to travel to Taiwan that arrived not by text or email but through my trusty fax machine at home. It was an unexpected invitation from Alex Wang in Taipei, inviting me to conduct a seminar and work with his skaters. While I had previously coached at workshops in Australia alongside international trainers, this would be my first solo endeavor, and I was both excited and a bit apprehensive. Nevertheless, I eagerly seized the opportunity and soon found myself in beautiful Taipei, hosted graciously by Alex and his skating club.

The humidity of Taipei struck me immediately upon arrival, a stark contrast to the conditions I was accustomed to. Skating outdoors wasn't something I had anticipated, but heavy rains soon forced us indoors, where we worked tirelessly at local schools' gymnasiums. Remarkably, none of the skaters complained; their enthusiasm and graciousness were inspiring.

Over those ten days, Alex and I put in intense effort, dashing around music stores and crafting multiple routines and classes. We were also invited to special luncheons at some of the city's most historic venues. However, I faced a challenge due to my sensitive stomach and dietary preferences—I am vegetarian and do not eat meat (that ended in 1995). Communicating this proved challenging at times, and I felt uneasy about not partaking in the main dishes served, which was seen as impolite for a guest of honor. Despite the cultural etiquette, I couldn't compromise on my dietary choices, which, truth be told, began as a bet with Charmaine back in 1990—that I couldn't go without meat for a week. Surprisingly, four years later, I was still a vegetarian.

We managed to squeeze in a performance at the opening of a new rink within an arcade complex in town. I opted for a low-key approach, wearing a simple black t-shirt and pants. I skated to a techno rendition of Vivaldi's Four Seasons, which resonated well with the mildly enthusiastic audience. It was an unforgettable experience, blending hard work with cultural immersion and the warmth of new friendships formed through a shared passion for skating.

I ventured into starting my own business, expanding on the students I had already taken under my wing. After a whirlwind trip to Nelson, New Zealand, with Kristen, Leanne, and Samantha Woodgate for International Trophy Day, a parent, Liz Innes, a New Zealander herself, approached me. With her eloquent charm, she asked if I'd be willing to give her daughter lessons back in Australia. They were keen to journey to Melbourne, and I was thrilled at the prospect.

Jacqui, who was only thirteen or fourteen then, visited for a few weeks with Liz and stayed at our home. We made some adjustments to ensure they felt comfortable, and soon, we all got on like a house on fire. Jacqui thrived among the other skaters at Rollerama, relishing the chance to train with them. I loved working with her—she was dedicated, intelligent, and always respectful. The perfect student!

JAYSON SUTCLIFFE

> *Each trip to Melbourne brought fresh and thrilling adventures, along with exciting new projects you were working on. I was continually inspired by your creativity, flair, passion, and unwavering dedication to "perfection." The choreography sessions, always recorded by 'Nonna Liz' for me to review back in New Zealand, were some of the best moments.*
>
> *I'll never forget those late nights spent watching you meticulously cut music on the mini-disc player, create incredible costumes in a matter of hours, or hanging out with Bev on the couch watching old skating videos while you took quick power naps before training. It always felt like a second home...*
> JACQUI INNES

This was also a fantastic opportunity for me to dive deeper into choreography. Creating routines for Jacqui year after year became something I eagerly anticipated, as did their visits. Liz treated me like her own son. We got along famously; her unique sense of humor, which not everyone appreciated, always had me in stitches.

Jacqui, meanwhile, loved shopping at all the outlets and brand stores here. She often left Australia with twice as much luggage as she arrived with. One of the greatest gifts from roller skating has been the lifelong friendships formed. I've watched Jacqui grow into a successful coach and loving mother, and we still spend time together. I consider them my family away from home and cherish them dearly.

> *When I asked Jayson in Nelson if we could come over for Jacqui to take some lessons, I never imagined we would stay with your family and end up feeling part of it! Early morning coaching at the Caribbean rink—lots of it—and always a 'fight' when it came to paying you for all those hours of work. Fortunately, I kept a notebook and knew what you were due! We watched all those fabulous Christmas shows you choreographed and all the props your father Colin made. What a dad, and what a sense of humor!*
>
> *My granddaughter calls me Nonna— a name that came from you. "Hurry up, Nonna," you'd say as I trailed behind you both. We always looked forward to several trips to Melbourne a year, staying as usual with the ever-accommodating Sutcliffes.*
>
> *You were a great coach, a fantastic friend to Jax, and the only 'son' I'll ever have...* LIZ INNES

To open the championship, I was asked to perform a demonstration. I was happy to do so, and for the privilege, I was one of the first people to skate on the stadium floor. After rolling around for a few minutes and getting a feel for it, I thought, "No way, I'm not skating on this." I'd had my time on the ice and wasn't about to restart again here! I thought of my students and all the other skaters who had to follow and compete; they would suffer equally. So, the prima donna in me came out, and I stood my ground. I went to the officials and politely asked them to clean the floor. It wasn't an option, apparently. So, I added,

> *If the floor isn't cleaned, I'm not skating tonight.*

With that said, mops and buckets appeared out of nowhere, and the floor was brought up to spec and in excellent condition for all of us. Winning!

Apart from teaching and coaching, I dedicated myself to full-time training, so I needed an income to support my choice. I always tried to train about three hours daily for figures and freestyle, pushing myself to the point where my feet were so irritated that standing became nearly unbearable. It was also a matter of what time was available at the rink or which venue I could use. I'm not sure how many athletes train alone, but since I was coaching during club practice times, my only option was to train during the day—by myself. It was never easy, and I did this for years, especially running through routines without encouragement or guidance and relying solely on pure motivation to nail the elements repeatedly.

Often, around lunchtime, Jamie and Margaret, the managers at Rollerama, would take their break in the café and watch me train. Their presence was a huge boost, and I always looked forward to performing a routine, hoping to catch their attention for a few minutes. Margaret, bless her heart, would get up, lean over the barrier, and cheer and clap for me, even spilling her sandwich in the process. She was the life of the party, and though she has sadly passed away, I can still hear her laughter echoing in the background when I skated around and around those figure circles. It always makes me smile.

Any athlete understands the disproportionate commitment required for a brief performance, but all this dedication culminates in just one four-minute program for skaters! This year, my performance approach leaned towards classical, rediscovering the profound beauty of my love for ballet. Given my preference for something slightly off-center, maintaining a classic yet subtly distinctive style led me to explore a new role: the choreographer.

The journey into choreography was serendipitous. While I'd been making up my routines for years, this had to be different. During a lunch break at the rink, I played music I'd cut together from the poignant original score of "Schindler's List," blending it with another piece by the co-composer Itzhak Perlman. I aimed to convey the story's symbolism on wheels in four minutes. As I practiced, two ladies who had just finished an adult morning class stood mesmerized by the music and my interpretation. I was also happy that somebody was interested in my training session. Out of politeness, I approached them to seek their opinion on my fledgling choreography. Fate intervened once more: they turned out to be seasoned choreographers. An eloquent and poised woman, Barbara had a daughter making waves in ballet. Suddenly, they had my full attention.

Inviting them onto the rink, we embarked on a collaborative journey. Delighted by the opportunity, we spent several hours brainstorming ideas and refining my envisioned routine. Their expertise in body lines and artistic expression helped me achieve remarkable results in a short period of time for the state meet.

Performing this routine often took me back to my teenage years in Adelaide, when I watched Scott Cohen live for the first time. I used to wonder what was going through his mind during those performances. Now, I think I finally understand what it means to skate, to be free, and to truly be yourself. It's easy to sit back and admire a mesmerizing performance, but knowing the depth and passion behind it has always been the essence of my journey, and I have Scott to thank for that.

> *The artistic part, I think, came from a lot of natural ability but also from watching myself and others. I gained ideas and admired various performances, but primarily, I learned from observing myself. Something that feels good often looks not so good, and I wanted to bridge that gap.*
>
> *I wanted to erase the line that restricted boys from being expressive and artistic without being considered 'fag' or 'homosexual.' I believed boys could interpret music and express themselves without stigma. Similarly, I thought girls should not be confined to just being artistic; they could be athletic, too. So, I wanted to blur that line and test the limits that had been carved out by the history of skating...* SCOTT COHEN

I premiered the new program at our state championships later that month in front of a surprisingly large audience. My co-choreographers sat eagerly in the front row, which, I suspect, contributed to some stage fright on my part. Adopting my opening position, kneeling with one arm raised and arched over my head and the other gently folded behind my back, I felt my legs tremble, and my arm weakened—typical nerves on opening night. The opening notes sounded, and as the melody filled the air, I lost myself in the music. All movements flowed automatically and effortlessly, resulting in what would be noted as my most emotional performance to date in Australia.

I often wondered how this would translate to a judge sitting center front of the stage, all eyes on you. But did it connect with them emotionally, or were they simply ticking boxes and being technical? I had tried and hoped to be different from the other male skaters of the era, notably in Australia, and it wasn't easy. Still, from what I had seen on videos earlier in my career as a young teen, things were starting to change, and I wanted to grow with that movement and not be left behind.

> *Jayson's skating performance was a fresh experience for us as judges because, before he came along, most of our male skaters focused on power-packed and masculine routines that often didn't relate to the music they were skating to. They performed their required elements with the music playing in the background, but Jayson tied everything together.*
>
> *His performance was more like watching a ballet, where all the movements were perfectly integrated with the music, making it feel like he was a part of it. He wasn't just executing the required elements with background music; his routines were arranged to interpret the music through his movements. This approach was unusual in the early 80s...*
> CAROL JESSOP (Judge).

ROLABOI, REVIVAL

My dear friend Melissa had been on a golden path to success since leaving roller sports eighteen months earlier. She had become one of Australia's most recognizable faces on television, starring in the popular drama "Home & Away" as Angel. Leading up to the 1994 National Championships, she surprised me with a call about featuring on the hit lifestyle show "The Great Outdoors," she wanted me to join her! It was an unbelievable opportunity to showcase our sport on national prime-time television, and they would film it at my new home, Caribbean Rollerama.

Melissa's appearance on the show did more for promoting our sport in that brief segment than anything I had ever done. I felt immense pride during the official filming. Despite her celebrity status, Melissa remained grounded, happily signing autographs and posing for photos with kids at the rink. When she put on her skates, everyone at the rink was captivated—astonished by her flawless execution of maneuvers she had perfected since childhood. People marveled at her as if witnessing the impossible. Since she hadn't skated in over a year, performing a double salchow jump side-by-side with her was impressive.

The night before filming, Mel and I had ventured out to a popular club in South Yarra, where she was bombarded with requests for her phone number. There was a massive queue outside the club, and we were freezing when we arrived, especially Melissa, who was scantily clad in a feather boa. However, as soon as the 'door bitches' spotted her, they opened the ropes and ushered us straight in! Around 3 am, it dawned on

Melissa that she had nothing to skate in for the segment. She stared at me blankly, "Oh my God," she screamed.

" *I don't have anything to skate in.* "

I wasn't sure if I had any material at home, but I assured her I would make something before our 8 a.m. rink call. It was already past 3 a.m., so we decided to call it a night and hang up our disco shoes. I got home around 4 a.m., utterly unfit for sewing! It was a chaotic moment. With just a few hours left before I had to be at the rink for filming, including getting some sleep, I had to sew like crazy.

To my relief, I found a few meters of black stretch velvet in my cupboard, leftover from outfits I had made for my students earlier that year. It wasn't just the obvious choice—it was the only one. I decided on a simple sleeveless bodysuit with leggings that would snugly fit over her white skates. I made it on the smaller side, knowing it would stretch to fit perfectly. Better a second skin than saggy crotch!

Interestingly, my sewing journey began because I complained to my mom about my pants being "baggy in the crotch," to which she replied, "Well, make them yourself." At fourteen, I took her advice and started learning. By the time I finished Melissa's outfit, I had managed only thirty minutes of sleep before rushing to shower and head to Rollerama for the shoot. Arriving at the rink, I felt incredibly rough. The hangover I had hoped to avoid caught up with me, and it was clear I was in no condition to perform. Yes, I had a few drinks that night, which was unusual for me, but it was enjoyable. As the crew began filming, they requested that I perform my routine, which sent shivers down my spine, given my condition. Nonetheless, I obliged, though I had to make frequent trips to the men's room for a breather, leaving me looking as pale as a ghost.

JAYSON SUTCLIFFE

> *We had some wild nights in Melbourne. Jay would dress me up in tiny feather outfits, and we'd go out to some crazy bars where we'd dance all night.*
>
> *One weekend, we went almost until the sun came up, and we had to be at the rink the next morning because I was shooting an episode of The Great Outdoors that included skating, and I didn't have an outfit, so Jayson made me an entire skating costume from scratch when we got home! He amazed me. He had no sleep, and I had a full costume.. MELISSA GEORGE*

Somehow, Melissa managed to appear as fresh-faced as any catwalk model! The outfit fit her perfectly, a fact I silently appreciated. Melissa's role in the shoot was straightforward. She portrayed her pleasant self, mingling with the public at the morning session in the rink, interacting with the camera, and sharing a few pointers and historical facts about roller skating. Later, Melissa and I attempted a few side-by-side elements. I even gave her an impromptu mock lesson on an inverted spin, which ended in laughter when it went hilariously wrong.

The cameramen also wanted some fast-paced shots among the crowd, so I crouched down, holding the heavy camera, and weaved through skaters on the rink, filming at ground level, while another skater pushed me from behind to maintain speed. The angles looked fantastic on playback, and the crew was pleased with the result—if only they knew how I felt inside!

The segment aired on 'The Great Outdoors' during the National Championships in Brisbane, accompanied by a story and photo of us in TV Week magazine. It was a fortunate timing that provided excellent publicity for the sport.

Despite becoming an international celebrity and starring in the US hit show "ALIAS," shortly after this shoot, Melissa has never lost touch with her former life as her career blossomed even further. Witnessing how much she had grown in such a short time was fantastic. Her full-time work in television and film, constantly under the spotlight, had broadened her horizons. Yet, she remained remarkably grounded, her genuine graciousness radiating like a golden aura around her. Melissa remains cherished as one of Australia's favorite daughters, even though she moved to live and work in the US in the years following.

A few months later, I landed in Milan once again. With a quiet smile, I breathed deeply, brimming with optimism as I embarked on another world championship. Italy was renowned for hosting spectacular events; this one in Salsomaggiore was no exception. Known as the town of health and beauty, Salsomaggiore is nestled 160 meters above sea level at the base of the rolling green Apennine hills, making it one of the most picturesque towns in northern Italy. The early mornings there were truly magnificent.

The championship drew large crowds, including many old friends I hadn't seen in years. Some were genuinely surprised I was still skating — if only they knew I competed until 2005! I also met a coach who was a brilliant dance skater, someone I had admired on video countless times: Billy Richardson. During my first training session, I noticed him watching me. While I was eager to show off my new choreography to the masses, my real goal was to impress him. After my session, he approached me with genuine kindness and praise. If only he knew how much I admired his skating. Then, he hit me with;

> *I love your style. You skate just like a 'dancer.'*

At the Palazzetto dello Sport, a cluster of large television screens adorned the front end of the skating arena, each spanning about 3x3 meters. While ideal for spectators seated high in the stands, they posed a challenge for athletes on the floor. Positioned at ground level, these screens broadcast live feeds during the events. This championship also saw Charmaine return to coaching me, providing the much-needed support and boost I sought. I was skating directly toward the screens as I approached the triple flip jump during my short program. Despite my focus, my mirrored image on the screen proved distracting at the critical moment before I executed the jump. I had no choice but to execute. Although I didn't land the jump cleanly, I managed to stay on my feet — a narrow escape from a potentially disastrous fall. It was a costly error;

in figure skating, any mistake in the short program can drastically impact your standings, a lesson I first learned in 1992 with a double axel mishap. Nonetheless, my scores remained consistently high, securing me the fourth position alongside my teammate Adrian Lomman, who closely followed in fifth — marking the first time two Australian skaters had achieved top-five positions at the world championship level.

Lee Taylor, Eric Anderson, and Heath Medeiros occupied the top three positions, and I knew Taylor lacked the technical prowess to prevent me from surpassing him for third place if we both performed well in the long program. Once again, the competition boiled down to Eric, Heath, and me. At least, I hoped.

Following complaints from several athletes, the main screen was turned off during the long programs. The quality varied widely in the men's event. Two new Italian competitors didn't match the standards set by their predecessors, Guerra or Kokorovec, so I didn't see them as serious threats. Mauro Mazzoni wasn't as strong as he had been the previous year. However, the surprise came from the newcomer from Argentina, Walter Iglesias, who sat in sixth position after an impressive short program. He posed a threat to those holding fourth and fifth places.

With the television screen darkened, the stadium filled, and several impressive performances already etched into the first half of the men's competition, the stage was set for the final contenders. Medeiros and Anderson delivered flawless programs, putting immense pressure with scores ranging from 9.6 to a perfect 10.0 across the board. Lomman, Taylor, and I awaited our turns. I felt primed and ready to step onto the rink, though Heath's perfect score of 10.0 only heightened the stakes.

Having already showcased my new routine to Schindler's List in Australia, I was eager to reveal my newfound passion for choreography. The silence was palpable as I knelt into position, awaiting the start of the music. Charmaine, Tammy, and Amanda stood in the marshaling area, breathing with me in solidarity. That said, they threw a challenge at me for this performance: to execute a signature Kylie/Uma Thurman pose as I passed by. Just moments before my triple flip, as I glided past them in the coaches' corner, I brushed my finger along my chin and smiled at the trio. Above the crowd and the music, I could hear them laugh.

With nothing to lose, every jump in the opening minutes of my performance ignited thunderous cheers from the crowd unlike any I had experienced before. It was electrifying, propelling me forward until... the moment the double axel arrived. Despite flawless execution thus far, fear crept in, and I opted for a safe double flip instead. Regrettably, I stumbled on the landing. It was a costly mistake, born of hesitation and a missed opportunity.

The judges' response to my performance elicited a mix of cheers and hushed anticipation in the arena. People scrutinized the scores, unsure of where they would place me. The marks were tightly grouped, ranging from 9.6 to 9.8. It was a varied outcome, but I knew it would edge me ahead of Taylor, who held third place—my immediate goal. Such tension creates a bittersweet atmosphere that fuels excellent competition.

Since 1992, Heath, Eric, and I have consistently occupied the top three spots in the world rankings. We have shared the podium numerous times, only swapping positions between Eric and me once. Heath consistently claimed the coveted crown, proving himself the strongest performer each year. He was truly unstoppable. However, Salsomaggiore marked Heath's final performance in his illustrious career, despite solid rumors of his return at the US Nationals in 1999.

Securing third place at this event felt like a victory, especially with the roaring support of the crowd throughout. Such appreciation, whether from a single spectator or a vast Italian audience, provided an adrenaline rush that made me feel like a true champion.

Upon our return to Australia, 'Priscilla Queen of the Desert' fever swept through town. I hadn't heard much about the movie before, but the concept intrigued me — drag queens trekking across the rugged Australian outback seemed like a must-see spectacle. As soon as it hit theaters, we rushed to watch it. We laughed uncontrollably; Guy Pearce, portraying a flamboyant young gay man in his twenties, stole the show with his tanned, buffed, and outrageously charming performance. The lake scene, where he dove into the water in knee-length pants, left Kathy Mason and me gasping for air. The costumes were sensational and became the inspiration for a group number I had to choreograph for an exhibition Christmas show.

I was working with a team of twelve girls for the performance, featuring eighty skaters. Each group's routine was themed around a theatrical production — musicals, plays, or films. It was irresistible to base our number on 'Priscilla.' After scouring Melbourne for supplies, Lisa Bishop and I found everything we needed, from meters of feather boas to ample fabric. We scheduled a day to work together, setting up a makeshift production line to start on the costumes. One day wasn't nearly enough to complete twelve intricate outfits, but it was a promising start. With the costumes underway, I began crafting the headpieces, thinking it would be straightforward. Surprisingly, it took nearly three weeks of dedicated effort to finish all twelve, but the results were stunning works of art that the girls loved. And it wasn't just the girls who loved them; a few outfits made their way to the infamous '3 Faces' nightclubs, worn by Sasha and Kathy. They were swamped by drag queens who were in awe, wanting to know where they had sourced the outfits. Kathy, of course, was the star of the number we put together with her glitz and no-limits approach to the character, living up to the Alicia Bridges line in the song, 'Oh, I love the Nightlife, I've got to Boogie.'

I chose not to perform with the girls in the Priscilla group. I didn't want to subject myself to the inevitable remarks and innuendos; the routine was always intended for the girls alone. Instead, my performance for the show was inspired by what many consider the greatest tragic epic: 'Phantom of the Opera.' My friend, Daniel Humphries, who is now a style guru, fashion writer, and publicist, informed me about props available from the Victorian State Opera. I was thrilled to discover I could access these revered relics — my goal was to find suitable items within our budget. The vast storage facility offered an array of props suitable for any production. It was ideal. I secured an incredible life-sized theatrical organ, identical to those in 'Phantom,' which served as the perfect centerpiece for my performance. Alongside it were stunning candelabras and a gondola on wheels, courtesy of my father, who spent hours creating the life-sized prop for us to sit and stand in.

The next challenge was to create the perfect ambiance to capture the mood and mystique of 'The Phantom,' which I had seen in London only weeks after the world championships. The Arts had such an impact on me as a skater, and I'm sure on many others as well. Going to the theatre evokes every creative cell in your body, filling you with a desire to perform.

Emerging from behind a black backdrop, we navigated through a dense cloud of smoke lit by eerie green floodlights. I appeared to steer the meticulously crafted gondola down the center of the floor alongside my partner, Kathy Mason, who sat gracefully in the front. She wore a stunning purple hooded robe over a shimmering pink silk gown, a remarkable find from her grandmother's wardrobe. The audience erupted into applause the moment we silently emerged.

JAYSON SUTCLIFFE

> " *I remember being asking to do "Phantom" with you, knowing it would be my last skating performance. It was emotional and fitting to finish my skating journey. Dragging out one of my nan's old satin ball gowns was perfect, and being pushed along the skating floor in a wooden gondola through the smoke, his dad made, was surreal. It was something that hadn't been done or dreamed of before—very you, always coming up with something unique and spectacular for the audience to marvel at...* KATHY MASON (CRETTENDEN) "

Clad in a full cape and mask, I disembarked from the gondola and parked it beside two softly glowing candelabras before rolling toward the grand organ at the stage's foot. The music began with the unmistakable and powerful theme from 'The Phantom.' As I commenced the performance, mimicking the actions of a masterful pianist, I briefly felt a glimpse of Sir Andrew Lloyd Webber's visionary world.

As the performance climaxed, Kathy dramatically tore the mask from my face. I instinctively recoiled and cowered, portraying the tortured character "Erik" as depicted in every interpretation of 'Phantom.' Arm-in-arm, Kathy and I then rolled towards the exit, receiving thunderous applause from the audience. The Phantom Exhibition stands as one of my all-time favorite showpieces. It was a spectacle of drama, with exquisite costumes and magnificently extravagant sets. Honestly, it was unlike anything I had done before. The only other showpiece that perhaps came close was my portrayal of 'Dracula' in a dramatic performance at the opening of a competition in January 1993, appearing from a coffin with fake extended fingers and vampire teeth, complete with fake blood oozing from my mouth as I rolled past the audience.

Dracula almost marked the first time my two worlds collided: figure skating and ballet. A good friend of mine, Andrew Bevarne, who has since sadly passed away, was at the Australian Ballet School. We became friends through mutual connections and a shared love of Kylie Minogue. He was just as passionate about her as I was. In a twist of fate, I soon discovered that he had two brothers back in Broken Hill who were also skaters. Although they were new to the sport, they were very active. It was uncanny and proved our friendship was meant to be. So, it became irresistible to perform without including him.

Emerging from a coffin, surrounded by mannequin heads and draped in black cloth, I skated by the audience, flashing my vampire teeth and sharp nails. The crowd's shrieks confirmed they were witnessing something entirely new. Shortly into the performance, Natalie Ambrose, dressed as a bride in a full-length black wedding dress, walked onto the rink, morbid and in character. Andrew soon followed, gliding onto the rink and pirouetting across the floor with a stunning display of dance, a stark contrast to the stiff figures we were used to seeing on skates.

Although it was an indulgent six-minute routine, we thrived on our explosion of impulsive creativity and passion, having made up the routine just hours before the opening.

And finally, the blood. I performed this routine a few times over that year, each time getting a feel for how to make more blood appear. At the opening of the 1993 Queensland championship, as I skated down the middle of the floor and spurted the fake blood from my mouth, there was so much that the floor had to be cleaned afterward. It was like a bloodbath and the death of that routine.

1993 was a year of exploration with demonstration routines. One that comes to mind and is possibly more controversial now than it was then occurred at the Mt Gambier competition. I participated in the 'Show Skate' event, a fun part of the competition that everyone entered. I wanted to shock the audience, and I figured there was only one way to do it: take off some clothes! The song "Male Stripper" came into my head and became a source of inspiration. When I committed to pulling it off, I found a trench coat, leather briefcase, rope, and a pair of... handcuffs. There was only one thing missing: a victim.

On the night of the performance, as the countdown from ten to one began, I rolled over to the guest judging panel, took Amanda and Tammy Bryant's lovely Nan, Iris, by the hand, and pulled her on stage to take a chair. Before she knew it, she was tied up and handcuffed, and I started to writhe around her, shaking my hips to the music. As the beat intensified, I dramatically removed my jacket, revealing a black vest and black satin pants. The crowd erupted in screams of laughter and cheers. But there was more. Seconds later, I grabbed my pants by the waist, tore them off, and whirled them around my head before hurling them into the air. Now bare-legged on skates, dressed in only a vest and swim trunks, I continued skating half-naked, performing jumps and spins.

The routine climaxed as I returned to Iris and sat on her lap. Despite the courageousness of the situation, Iris was a good sport. She laughed and gave me a perfect score of 10.0, just like the other two judges. She even quipped,

> *You're gonna have to sit me down; I need a cuppa tea after that!*

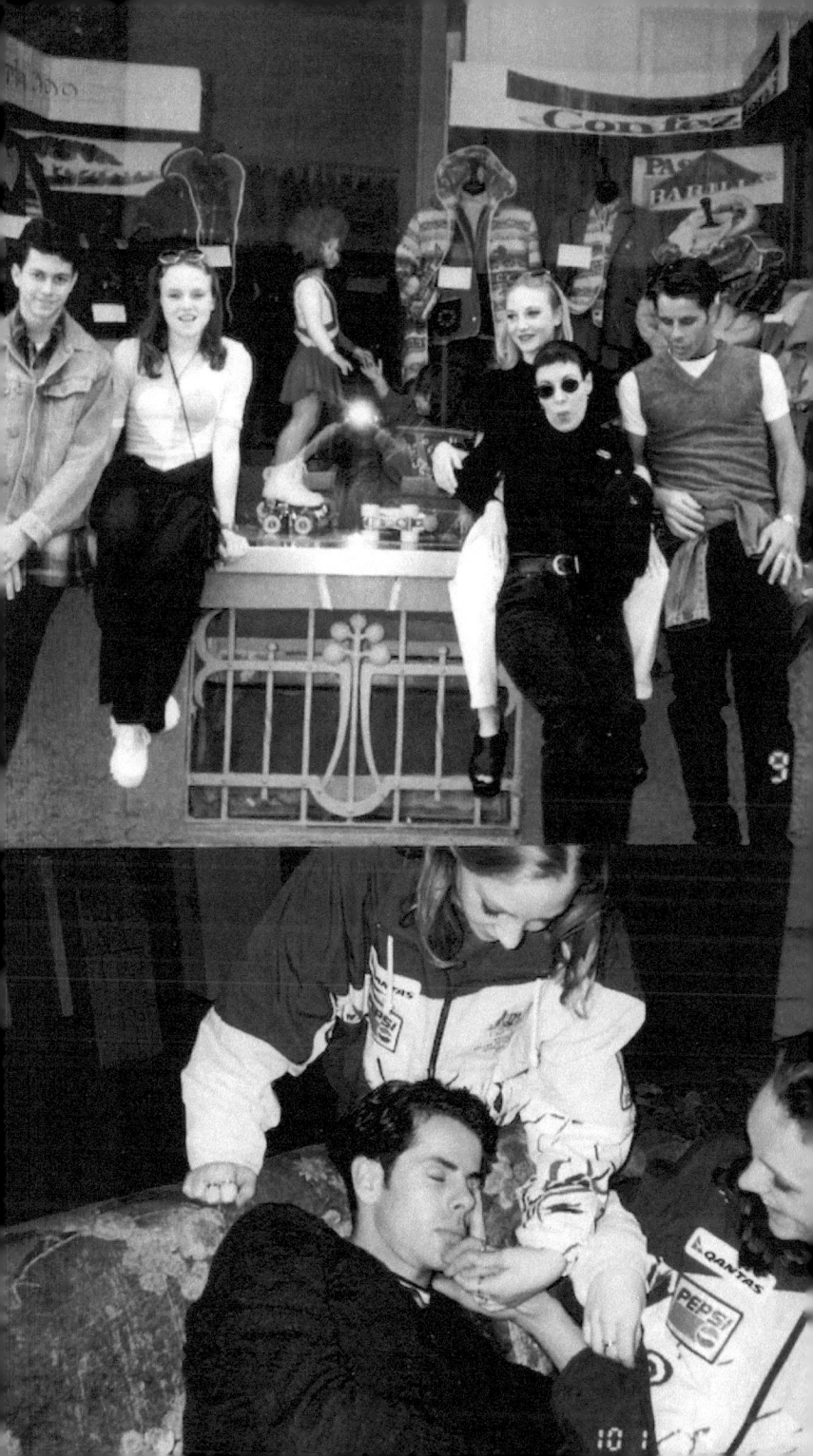

Jayson Sutcliffe... one of the top three artistic skaters in the world.

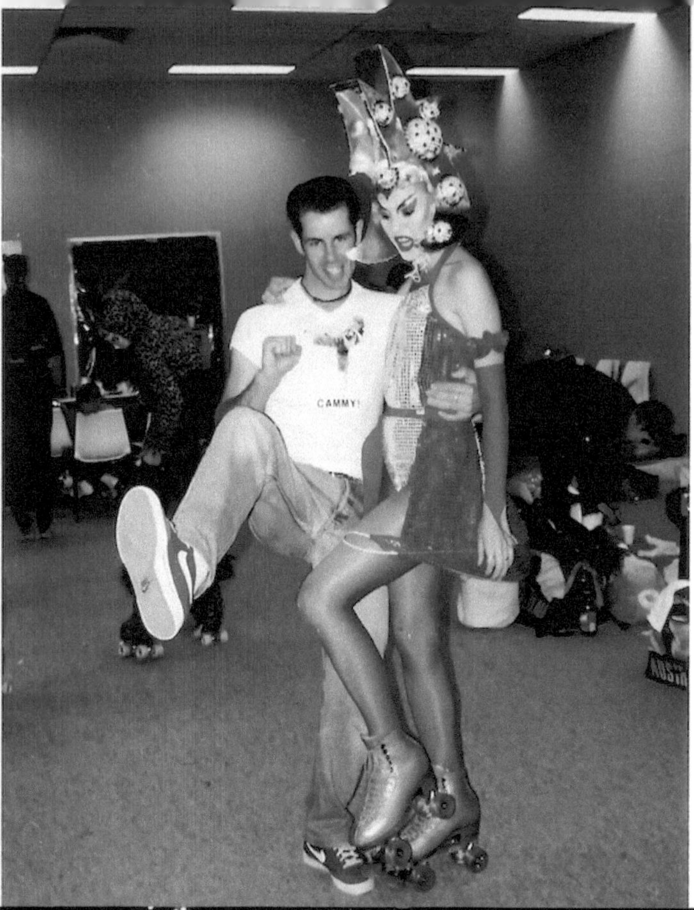
CAMMY!

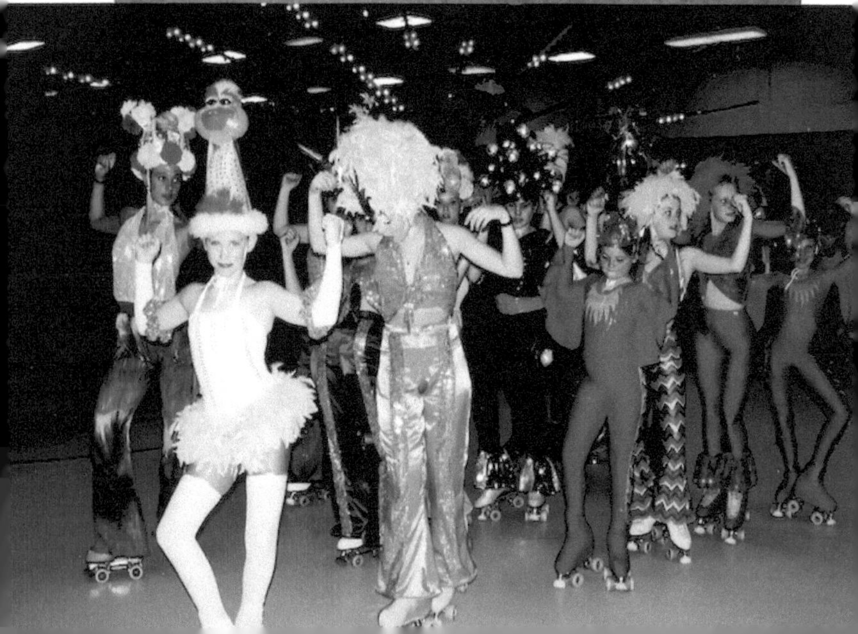

'Would you still be proud of me if I was gay?'

13

PAVING THE WAY

By 1995, I was entering my tenth year on the international circuit. Even though I had competed in nine world championships and won seven medals in the past five years, the elusive GOLD medal still hadn't come my way. Questions started creeping into my mind:

"When will this journey conclude?"

"What is considered enough?"

"How much longer can I sustain this?"

Will I ever be a world champion?

While I maintained a deep passion for my sport and didn't feel ready to walk away, I also recognized that I needed to broaden my horizons beyond roller sports. I sat down and mapped out my aspirations for the upcoming year. Financial challenges quickly emerged as a primary concern. Although I received some support from the Australian Institute of Sport and the Australian Sports Commission, it was modest at best — insufficient to secure my future. Their assistance primarily covered international travel requirements, leaving me reliant on the aid of my parents and supporters through fundraising efforts. Direct assistance from the Federation was lacking, with funding primarily sourced from government grants and local councils.

Included in my immediate goals, I scheduled a trip to the German Cup in May. I faced a decision between competing in Freiburg and attending the Oceania Championships, conveniently located minutes away from my home at the Springer's Leisure Center. Australian team competitions followed a cost-sharing approach, requiring a payment of up to $900 to participate locally. Based on this, I declined the invitation to the Oceania Championships and opted for Germany instead. Although attending the international meet would exceed $900 in expenses, I saw it as an opportunity to perform in front of world-class judges and compete against top-tier athletes.

The Australian hierarchy didn't support my decision to prioritize the European competition over the locally organized championships. This decision further strained my already uneasy relationship with many officials. They viewed me as rebellious, a renegade skater, without considering how the German meet could benefit my athletic development and, consequently, the sport as a whole. Their primary concern was that their top athlete needed to be supporting national events. On the flip side, I understood the value of the Oceania Championships in preparing athletes aspiring to compete internationally. Still, it offered little advantage to those like myself who were already seasoned in world-level competition.

It's disheartening that roller sports in Australia and many other parts of the world receive little promotion for excellence. Media and managers thrive on the importance of role models in other sports. Swimming wouldn't capture the same attention without figures like Michael Klim, Kieren Perkins, Hayley Lewis, Ian Thorpe, and Grant Hackett. Imagine Australian tennis without Leighton Hewitt, Pat Rafter, or Mark Philippoussis — they embody the sport and promote and ignite interest among future generations. Their success translates into lucrative endorsements, bolstering the sport's image through media and management efforts.

> *The Federation didn't recognize the elite skaters and treated them like ordinary ones. Instead of being celebrated as world champions, as they are overseas, they received no special acknowledgment here. I don't think it's fair because Jayson and Tammy represented Australia and brought home medals, lots of them, yet received no thanks for their achievements... Mom.*

Despite Australia's achievements in becoming world champions in Artistic and Speed skating events, the average person on the street may not even know that roller sports are serious disciplines. Australia needs a strategic business plan to further develop our sport before it fades into obscurity. Despite my initial inclination to broaden my horizons, my focus returned to the sport — and winning. And win, we did...

Tammy Bryant and I emerged victorious in our free skating events in Freiburg at the German Cup, with an added bronze in figures securing me the silver medal overall in the combined event. My student Kristen achieved third place in her division, a remarkable feat considering she was initially placed in the wrong age group at her first international competition, competing against 14-year-olds at just 12. Each division boasted over ten skaters, creating fierce competition and reinforcing my ongoing advocacy for Australia to send its top athletes to such events consistently.

At the German Cup, another 14-year-old captured everyone's attention: Italy's newest star, Luca D'Alisera. Competing in the Cadet Boys Free Skating event, he flawlessly executed a double axel and a triple toe loop—remarkable feats for someone his age. His performances were not only technically impressive but also showcased extraordinary artistry. Under the guidance of his trainer, Gabriele Quirini, Luca was clearly part of an unstoppable team destined for greatness.

Gabriele, of course, became one of the most successful coaches ever, with his students winning over 38 world titles. Tragically, in March 2018, Gabriele was killed in a motor vehicle accident in Italy. His death was a terrible loss for the skating world and for me personally, as he was a dear friend and mentor to many.

After the ceremony, I asked Luca if he'd like to perform a side-by-side jump for our video camera. Shy and nervous, he reminded me of my younger self meeting Cohen at 14. Despite his humility, Luca was already a star, though he hadn't realized it yet. We skated around the rink together and initially fumbled our first attempt at the triple jumps, drawing a crowd. On our second attempt, we nailed it, exchanging fist pumps in triumph. It was a personal highlight for me, and as history has shown, Luca has become one of the most iconic and legendary skaters in history.

Our victories in Freiburg significantly boosted Tammy's and my confidence as we prepared for upcoming National and World meets. Securing the title also played a crucial role in obtaining financial support from the government. Any international success, especially a win at a prestigious event like the German Cup, substantially impacts securing funding. My sights were now set on Spain for the next challenge.

ROLABOI, REVIVAL

The President of the Spanish Skating Federation graciously invited me to participate in an upcoming exhibition night in Barcelona, and I eagerly accepted. It would be my first time visiting Spain, and with a few days to spare after Freiburg, I planned to arrive early. Eric Anderson, who had also arrived early from the US, joined me. With time on our hands, we decided to explore the city, perhaps have a drink or play pool. Little did we know our plans would take a humorous turn.

As we leisurely wandered through the city, we stumbled upon a small, somewhat seedy-looking bar that strangely caught our interest. Stepping inside, we hadn't even ordered our first drink when a couple of older women approached us. The situation seemed dubious, especially considering they appeared old enough to be our mothers. Unable to speak Spanish, I was utterly clueless about what was happening, but it seemed we had unwittingly positioned ourselves as obvious tourists ripe for some kind of scam.

They asked us to buy them a few drinks, and I figured, why not? Once they realized we were willing to spend, they quickly tried to separate us, hinting at engaging in the oldest profession known to man. This proposition held zero appeal for me; even Eric, known for his charm, seemed unenthusiastic. The idea of being undressed by one of them had me shaking in my boots, with only one thought in mind: "Get me out of here!"

Attempting to leave, we were halted by the bartender demanding eighty US dollars. We hadn't finished our first drinks or engaged with the women, who undoubtedly factored into the inflated charge. Eric struggled to explain in broken

Spanish, floundering like a fish out of water. He managed to negotiate the bill down to $40, a small price for a tale that still leaves us laughing hysterically.

Fun in Barcelona - Eric, Eva, Jayson, Heidi and Clementé

A couple of days later, the rest of the top skaters began to arrive. The team included Patrick Venerucci, Beatrice Rossi, Mauro Mazzoni, Antella Parada, Eva Ambros, and a select group of talented artists from Italy and Spain to round out the group. As usual for such events, early mornings were dedicated to rehearsals. We all rolled up to the stadium, only to discover, much to our horror, that the floor was as slippery as ice. No wheel on the market could have prevented us from slipping. It was a nightmare, but as professionals, we had to find a way to make the show go on. I briefly recalled the

Ajax incident and wondered if a similar technique might be employed successfully here.

By evening, the streets surrounding the stadium were packed with spectators. Around three thousand eager attendees scrambled to their seats, anticipating the performances we had in store for them. Eric, always one for a prank, couldn't resist teasing the girls by throwing flowers at them once the doors opened.

> *I remember throwing the flowers out the door to the people waiting. You would have thought I was throwing giant steaks at 100 lions who hadn't eaten in months. They ripped them up in seconds, fighting for them! ... Eric Anderson.*

The floor conditions provided plenty of entertainment. While sitting on the sidelines, we amused ourselves by betting on who could complete their performance without slipping. Unfortunately for Mauro, his performance was abruptly cut short when his rubber toe stop came loose in less than thirty seconds. The look of dismay on his face was truly priceless.

My exhibition featured the original score from 'Interview with The Vampire' and another rendition of a short program set to the music of 'Legends of The Fall.' As Spain's TVE broadcast artistic roller skating live to hundreds of thousands of viewers, back in Australia, millions sat in their recliners with a beer in hand, engrossed in their usual dose of footy. At that moment, though, football, cricket, and other sports were the farthest things from my mind. We were performing at the 'Palau Blaugrana' in front of a packed house, and the crowd loved it.

As the night drew close, the audience reached a fever pitch. Many teenage fans stood in the stands, screaming and causing absolute chaos. They were determined to grab our attention one last time! Despite attempts by stadium staff to calm them down and clear the building, the chanting and clapping persisted relentlessly. Most enthusiastic youngsters, predominantly girls, hoped for a final glimpse of the skaters or even an autograph despite our descent to the changing rooms below.

The adoration from the spectators was overwhelming. Eventually, after the last die-hard fans were escorted out, we were quietly whisked away through a rear exit to our transport. It was a well-intentioned but unsuccessful effort to make our departure swift and unnoticed.

I had expected a quiet departure from the building, but reality was far from that. As soon as the rear door swung open, we were engulfed in a surreal and sensational moment. People surged towards us from all sides, excitedly shrieking and tugging at our clothes. Their hero worship was intense, and each fan was eager to capture the moment on film or as a souvenir. Pens were wielded like weapons, darting in every direction.

Eric was just a few steps away, and I caught his bewildered glance. We had both performed in front of appreciative crowds before, but nothing had prepared us for this. That night, I experienced what it must feel like to be a rock star, faced with an overwhelming frenzy of girls (and boys) crying, screaming, pushing, and shoving to catch a glimpse of us. It was the kind of hysteria typically associated with Hollywood celebrities. I was left dazed and bewildered, a sensation that lingered with me for days.

We hurried through the crowds towards the waiting cars as swiftly as possible. The drivers shouted urgently for us to hurry, clearly concerned for our safety. Eric, always a favorite with the adoring fans, couldn't resist lingering to savor the moment – after all, we were young, and such experiences were rare.

Once safely crammed into the backseats of the waiting cars, the drivers peeled away, showing little regard for the crowd's safety. They powered through the masses, eager to exit the arena's perimeter quickly. I cherish the final glimpses I caught of those fans: girls hugging, tear-streaked faces, and waves of farewell bidding us into the sanctuary of darkness.

Back home, my focus remained steadfast. I had clinched victories at the German Cup and our National meet, diligently adhering to my rigorous training regimen. A new addition to my routine was setting up a video camera during practice sessions. Placing it atop a garbage bin in the middle of the rink, I'd hit record and skate off, ensuring my triple flip jumps were captured for later detailed analysis. With no coach present, the camera became my most invaluable tool, pinpointing areas for improvement and refining my technique. Today's kids have no idea how fortunate they are to have access to such advanced technology and the opportunity to learn from anyone, anywhere, at any time. I would have cherished that kind of access back in my day.

My performances were promising, signaling that I was on course for success in Colombia come December. Could this upcoming world meet be where I finally achieved my lifelong dream? Would all the dedication and sacrifices culminate in that pivotal moment? Would I hear those words, "And the Champion of the World is…" Could it finally be me?

It had been four years since my brother Colin passed away. Each day remained a challenge, especially for my mom, who continued to mourn his loss and grapple with the tragedy. I struggled to comfort her, unsure how to provide her solace. More often, she selflessly worried about my well-being and what I needed to succeed in my sport. Despite our arguments and disagreements, deep down, like all mothers, she only wanted what was best for me—ultimately, a gold medal on the mantel.

While achieving that goal was paramount to her, I was still wrestling with being open about my sexuality. At 25, I was still partially in the closet, at least to my parents. I had confided in Colin about being gay before he passed, and his acceptance and encouragement to embrace my true self resonated deeply with me. Yet, despite his support, I continued to feel constrained, yearning to break free from pretending to be someone I was not. I suspect both of my parents knew deep down I was gay but chose never to make anything of it. I blame myself for not being more upfront earlier about it and confronting my fears, to be honest about it.

ROLABOI, REVIVAL

On top of that, there was still a hint of uncertainty, the pressure building silently at the back of my mind about my abilities. Strangely enough, one person came to mind.

I soon found myself strolling through the CBD of Melbourne, making my way to a prominent hotel where I knew I would encounter someone I hadn't seen in years. Upon entering the hotel, I unexpectedly ran into a friend—none other than the boy I had kissed at a nightclub long ago. It felt oddly fated, and we exchanged numbers. Then, to my side, there he was... Mark Lind. He was reprimanding a young hotel staff member. He had risen to the role of manager. When he noticed me, his expression was ambiguous—neither delight nor despair. It was too late, despite my uncertainty about being there; he was already approaching me.

We exchanged pleasantries, and I sensed he could see that I was seeking some form of validation, perhaps reassurance that I could achieve greatness.

"So, what's up? You must need something. Otherwise, you wouldn't be here, right?"

Like always, he was blunt. He knew of my accomplishments but attributed them to our past association, offering to assist me again. At that moment, I realized I didn't need his approval or validation when he reached over the table and touched my hand. After fifteen minutes of listening to him, I understood that I had outgrown any need for his influence and that I was better off without him.

On the morning of our departure for Colombia, as I packed my bags, my mom entered my room with freshly laundered clothes. We shared a moment, and she reassured me, "No matter what happens in Colombia, I'll still be proud of you." I felt confident about my prospects and wondered if she shared the same optimism. Suddenly, almost without thinking, I blurted out;

> *Would you still be proud of me if I was gay?*

Her expression froze momentarily. I said it, I actually said it, and I am unsure if I expected any response, but she hugged me tightly and said, "We would discuss it when I returned home." Uncertain whether her response was acceptance or denial, I left it at that. I still wasn't sure she accepted who I was, but it was a step in the right direction and a huge weight lifted from my shoulders. Then she said, "I still love you, no matter what."

Before our flight to Colombia, the Australian team met in Sydney for a brief training session at the Tarren Point roller rink. Despite its brevity, I was eager to showcase my progress on a triple loop; a jump rarely attempted in competitions during those days. While not part of my competition program, I aimed to have it as a potential 'head-fuck' for my competitors at the official training sessions. Performing it under pressure was challenging, but I wanted to be prepared.

The flight was exceptionally long and exhausting. Enduring such a journey across the world tests one's stamina, but this flight felt interminable. Due to scheduling constraints, we even had to overnight in Miami. By the time we reached Colombia, we were exhausted, only to encounter another setback upon arriving at Bogotá airport—a five-hour delay awaiting a connecting domestic flight to Bucaramanga.

Everyone was growing increasingly restless, a mix of fatigue and concern about our safety in the airport. Several groups were lingering around, and the lounge felt crowded with hundreds of aimless wanderers. I was particularly wary about security and my luggage, having had my fair share of lost items. Sitting idle drove me mad; I felt my circulation slowing down.

JAYSON SUTCLIFFE

That was when I decided I needed to move. I pulled my skates from my hand luggage, put them on, and began skating around. As soon as I did, I heard Amanda Bryant in the distance, saying, "Oh-yah!" We laughed! It was something we often said to each other, never without laughter. It was pretty unusual to see someone skating in an airport, especially in full Australian Team attire, which caught the attention of the armed guards. I asked if I could take a photo with them to prevent any issues. Seeing us posing together brought big, amused smiles to their faces, and I avoided getting arrested.

> *As I collected my bags from the carousel and made my way over to the rest of the Australian team, who were gathered in an open area of the Bogotá airport, I saw we were waiting to board another flight to Bucaramanga, our destination, and I had no idea what was yet to unfold there.*
>
> *Some team members were sleeping on rows of chairs, eating, reading, or stretching on the floor. But not Jayson! When I glanced over at him, I saw he had retrieved his skates from his bag and was now skating around the Bogotá airport. As I sat back, watching him in disbelief, I quickly realized he was choreographing parts of the routine he would be performing at the world championships...*
> AMANDA BRYANT

Finally, we made our way towards Girón, Bucaramanga. As our journey continued down a sloping road, we observed the standard of the local homes with a mix of surprise and disbelief. It certainly was an eye-opener and nothing like Bogotá. I thought, "Wow! It's so boiling here. I can't believe we have to skate in this heat" before considering the living conditions.

There was a brief silence on the bus as we all leaned back and reflected on what we took for granted back home. For those with limited travel experience, confronting the stark reality of third-world living standards can be profoundly eye-opening. Witnessing homes constructed from mere sheets of corrugated iron and cardboard boxes, similar to what I had seen in Jakarta, evokes strong emotions. It seems unjust and almost incomprehensible that people still endure such conditions in the modern era.

Throughout the journey, I maintained a contemplative silence, pondering the level of poverty and challenges faced here. In contrast, our main preoccupation was competing for a world title. When visiting cities like Bucamaranga, you're guaranteed to encounter untold stories of harsh living conditions, far removed from the comforts of a five-star hotel lobby. As I explored the street markets for artifacts and handmade gifts, I met many locals from the villages. They eagerly shared the stories behind their wares, their enthusiasm almost childlike despite the challenging circumstances. I couldn't help but look at them with empathy, wondering where they found the resilience to endure such sweltering, unforgiving heat.

In contrast to the city's hardships, the luxury of a large sunken pool outdoors at our hotel was a welcome relief. We took full advantage of it whenever possible. Usually, I'm not a fan of swimming, especially at the beach; I'm more comfortable in clean water where I can see the bottom—though admittedly, swimming isn't my strong suit. Yet, I was more than willing to take the plunge in that heat.

Our first encounter with the local television media happened poolside. Upon learning that the first teams had arrived, they swiftly arrived at our hotel for interviews. Eager to represent, I volunteered to speak with them. When they asked where I was from, I cheekily pointed to the back of my swimsuit, proudly displaying "Australia." They found it amusing, and that night, I felt oddly honored to see my swimsuit-clad backside featured in the sports headlines. We quickly became favorites with the news team, often appearing in event highlights and promotional spots. It shows that being cooperative with the media can pay off! Being nice also helps.

Early in the week, I encountered a young skater named Diego Farina from Argentina. He earned the nickname 'Calvin' for resembling a 'Calvin Klein model'. I discovered that Diego had been a fan of mine for many years, and his favorite performance was my 'Edward Scissorhands' program in Tampa '92. I thought that was cool. So, we adopted him as one of us!

JAYSON SUTCLIFFE

> *When I was 13 years old, there wasn't a spare moment during breakfast, lunch, dinner, or any other spare time that I didn't spend watching videos of Jayson's routines at different world championships, and although the world skating scene was also dominated by some other great skaters, mostly Americans, and Italians, to me, watching Jayson skate had always meant something completely different.*
>
> *He exerted, and still has, some mixed sensations every time he is on the floor, of pleasure, fascination, and awe... frankly, there isn't any point in singling out just one of these emotions because his skating provoked many others indeed. He was the ideal, perfect skater in my mind. In fact, he was the skater I wanted to become... Diego Farina.*

I was deeply flattered by Diego's words and admired his courage to express his admiration face-to-face at such a young age. It's not every day someone tells you you're their idol, at least not in my experience. For so long, I had looked up to the elites like Cohen, Guerra, and McGuire, admiring their skill and hoping to reach their level. Then, one day, something shifted—I decided I didn't just want to be like them; I wanted to beat them. And that's when everything changed.

Diego and I have been close friends ever since. It reminded me of when I first met Scott Cohen when I was fourteen. Diego eventually stopped skating in 2000 to pursue modeling and full-time studies, but we've stayed connected through daily online interactions, and I cherish our bond like that of brothers.

As the junior championships kicked off, Kristen competed, coinciding with her 13th birthday. She qualified alongside Rachael Sketcher and Emma Ramsey, all making their debut at their first Junior World Championship. It was a significant moment for them as they embarked on their international skating journey.

Kristen's performances in Colombia were solid, earning her a 10th-place finish, a goal she had set before we departed from Australia. As her coach, I couldn't have been prouder, especially considering the strong field of over 30 skaters. Kristen's mom, Mary, shared in this pride, reflecting on how far Kristen had come in just three years to compete on the world stage.

At the same time, the senior teams arrived and started training at a different venue. Despite the sweltering heat, which often soared to 35-38 degrees Celsius, we could sense our preparation was strong, notably that of Tammy and Amanda Bryant; the girls were on fire, and not because of the extreme temperatures. The heat limited our training sessions to only about 20-30 minutes on the rink. Would this be enough to keep us in top shape for the upcoming battles against the world's best? Only time will tell.

'Everyone knew we were the ones to beat'

14

THE LONG ROAD TO THE TOP

During the junior competition of the 1995 World Championship, every event drew a full house, including the training sessions. Daily media coverage generated significant interest in the event, contributing to an electrifying atmosphere for the hundreds of athletes worldwide. Each morning, I would walk up the dirt road to the reception area of our hotel, eagerly searching through the local newspapers for sports headlines or articles about the championships. I hoped to find mention of myself at some point so that I could bring home a clipping for my mother as a cherished memento. Print media coverage of roller skating was rare, making each discovery even more special. By the end of our eleven days in Colombia, I had amassed about forty pages of clippings.

Competition time approached for the senior teams. As the days, hours, and minutes ticked by, the anticipation grew—the main event never far from our minds. Usually, I would have nervously anticipated the competition, with butterflies fluttering in my stomach. But in Bucamaranga, I found myself strangely calm, almost eerily so. I couldn't recall being so relaxed right before a world championship, not since 1990.

To maintain that sense of calm, I stuck to my routine: attending training sessions, spending time at the venue supporting others, and returning to the hotel for a swim and hanging out with Alan Dowsett and Craig Barry. Despite knowing it wasn't ideal for an athlete, I indulged in a bit of sunbathing, a favorite pastime shared with Jonelle McKane and Amanda Bryant. The hotel's cuisine was a highlight, especially a dish called 'baby beef'—tender, garlic-infused meat that melted in my mouth under the Colombian sun. Paired with fries or salad, it became my daily go-to meal.

Dinner times were often filled with laughter and camaraderie. Tammy Bryant frequently reminds me of when I supposedly tipped a bowl of spaghetti over her head. I can't quite recall the incident clearly, or perhaps I choose not to, but Tammy insists it happened, and her recounting always brings laughter to our conversations.

The official training sessions went exceptionally well as we approached the short program competition. In the first session, I decided to implement my first shock tactic and attempt the triple loop jump I had been diligently working on leading up to Colombia. Ever since witnessing Eric Anderson perform one in Spain during practice sessions at the exhibitions, landing this jump had become a personal goal to prove my readiness for the challenges ahead. Eventually, I aimed to incorporate the triple loop into my competition program. When Eric saw me successfully land one, he skated past me, whispering with a smile,

> *You bastard!*

What a legend! It just proves that skaters can be great friends and great competitors at the same time, no matter the outcome, and Eric was just that. Year after year, we competed fiercely for medals, yet at the end of the day, we could always return to the hotel, share a drink, laugh about the day's events, and then be back in the arena the next day, ready to battle for medals all over again.

> *There was a certain buzz in the air at every Australian Team training session. All the other competitors from around the world would come to watch the Australians train as we were nailing everything. We were at the peak of our careers, and everyone knew we were the ones to beat...*
> AMANDA BRYANT

I found the conditions of the floor to be favorable—a freshly polished wooden surface that felt like gold under my skates despite its size being far within the minimum international requirements. It reminded me a lot of the Youth Hall, where we skated in 1988. The size was almost identical.

Back then, I used to complain about it constantly, and now, here I was, aiming to win a world title on a rink of the same size. It's funny how perspectives change over time. My thinking was, "This floor is smaller, but it's hotter. That means I won't be skating hard and using less energy." In some sense, it meant I'd be covering less floor space, and it did agree with me for once.

The stadium in Bucamaranga had been finished just before our arrival, lacking windows and air conditioning. However, I was surprisingly adapting well to the heat, having been in town for nearly two weeks and acclimatizing gradually. Coming from the beginning of an Australian summer likely gave me an added advantage in adjusting to the Colombian climate. Either way, it was still incredible to be back at worlds and seeing all of my skating family from other countries, but there was just never enough time to spend with them.

> *Jayson as a team member was a challenge, bloody hell. When you're managing a team, especially in a foreign country, you want everyone to stay united and work closely together. The problem with Jayson was that he knew people from every other country at the championships. Trying to keep him with the team, having him sit with us and cheer for our people, was incredibly difficult. Trying to get Jayson to do anything was like hurting bloody cats... CHRIS CLOUGH (TEAM MANAGER)*

ROLABOI, REVIVAL

Security was exceptionally tight everywhere we went in Bucamaranga. Each national team had assigned guards who shadowed us daily from 6 am to 12 am, rotating in shifts. Surprisingly, many of these guards were cadets not yet 16 years old, fully armed and assertive in their roles. Given compulsory national service in the military for 15-year-old males, their presence wasn't uncommon, though it was striking to see such young individuals wielding authority. The public respected their fortified presence, acknowledging their authority despite their age. Despite their serious role, they were friendly and even allowed us to pose with their weapons for a few snapshots.

Tammy was the first of Australia's top contenders to compete, and she lived up to expectations, dominating the short program and securing a significant lead—yes, that's right, the top spot! This marked Tammy's first time ranking in the top 3 after the short program in her five appearances at a World Championship. Her success motivated me, as I knew she was moving closer to achieving my goal of becoming a world champion. Her sister Amanda also performed incredibly well, finishing in fifth place despite a slight error on an inverted spin, a class 'A' spin she is typically known for—a moment she vividly recalls to this day.

I sat in the stands during Tammy's performance with her mother, Yvonne. We cheered wildly as she completed her routine, confident she would secure the top spot. While thrilled for Tammy, my earlier calm demeanor began to waver as I started to feel anxious about my upcoming performances and questioned,

> *How was I going to live up to this?*

My short program took place the following night on what was likely the muggiest, hottest evening since our arrival. Despite wearing a short-sleeved outfit, the black PVC material on the shoulders and sleeves caused me to sweat profusely. Nevertheless, I began my program strongly and executed my triple flip flawlessly.

"Yes," I whispered to myself.

> *That's all the hard work done now. Just keep your cool and skate hard.*

I should have known better. You never, ever, ever become complacent, over-confident, or assume. The moment I did that, I missed the take-off for the triple salchow in my following combination. I was pissed off at myself for making such a silly mistake, something I landed flawlessly in practice every day. This time, it wasn't the double axel giving me trouble. It was a costly error that left me once again in fifth place. I felt like I had let down my teammates, myself, and my parents.

However, I was determined and more prepared than ever. I knew I could make a significant impact in the long program. Historically, your placement in the long program often determines the overall outcome, as I had proven in previous years when I moved from sixth place to second. I was confident that if I gave it my all in the long program, I could improve from fifth place and finally achieve my dream of standing atop the podium with a gold medal around my neck. Forty-eight hours to go…

Argentina's Walter Iglesias was leading after the first round. I didn't believe his technical skills would sustain him in the final to hold onto the number one position, but I knew better than to make assumptions. Eric Anderson was also in the top three, posing as a formidable opponent for the long program, especially to Walter.

As the anticipation and tension mounted for Tammy's long program, we could sense victory in the air. We were confident she was on the brink of becoming the World Champion. The Australians erupted with joy from the first moments of her program, witnessing her dream unfold before their eyes. Tammy flawlessly executed each element, powering through without faltering until the end. As composed as ever, Charmaine stood to the side, barely blinking. Tears streamed down my face alongside Tammy's mother, Yvonne, and the entire Australian team by the three-minute thirty mark of her four-minute performance. Once again, I stood in my seat, jumping and screaming in ecstatic support for her.

When Tammy finished her program, I rushed down the stands and embraced her with a big hug. Amanda, Charmaine, and I enveloped Tammy in a collective outpouring of admiration and love. She had achieved it. Tammy Bryant was Australia's first world champion. Who could not feel any prouder?

> *My sister, Tammy, and I had trained so hard that year. We lived and breathed skating for hours and hours every single day working up to this moment. Having skated her heart out, Tammy had taken out the 1995 Ladies World Championship GOLD medal. Australia's first...* AMANDA BRYANT

Following the presentation ceremony at the stadium, the celebrations were somewhat subdued at the hotel because many other team members still had their competitions ahead. It was bittersweet, as Tammy had clinched the championship, and Amanda had made a remarkable leap to fourth place after a stellar long program. There were murmurs that Amanda deserved third; we all believed it and knew it, but it seemed unlikely that two sisters from Australia would both be on the podium. Still, it was a night destined for celebration, although Tammy, as humble and modest as she is, was happy to go to bed.

> *I never imagined that I would be the first Australian to win a gold medal—I always thought Jayson would be. The only thing I did differently in 1995 compared to other years I competed at worlds and trained for them was making a deal with myself right at the start of the year. I told myself that if I wanted to win the world championships, I had to be significantly better than everyone else. There couldn't be any reason for the judges to place another skater ahead of me... TAMMY BRYANT*

However, the festivities would have to wait until after the competition. By then, I hoped not just to celebrate for Tammy but also with her. Later that night, I sat by the pool with Charmaine and confided in her about my nervousness, especially about living up to Tammy's standard. Charmaine, ever supportive, reiterated her belief that,

JAYSON SUTCLIFFE

" *What's meant to be will be.* "

Her words were a comforting reminder during my apprehensions. I went back to my hotel room and tried to sleep. The fire inside me burned brighter than ever. As I lay in bed, a whirlwind of thoughts raced through my mind. Instead of sleeping, I visualized my performance, rehearsing every element flawlessly. The mental rehearsal felt so vivid that I even felt goosebumps, imagining that moment of perfection on the rink.

At first light, I was filled with energy and excitement. I started my day with a refreshing swim in the pool, though my version of a few laps is more like playful splashing. After a hearty breakfast, I prepared to head to the stadium with Charmaine. Her quiet words of wisdom always struck a chord with me, giving me the strength and belief I needed. It was my turn.

During my final practice session before the big event, I spontaneously decided to tweak my program. Instead of opening with a simple double axel, I opted for a more challenging double axel, loop, and triple toe loop combination. It was a risky move since I had never attempted this combination in competition before, but to my surprise, I executed it flawlessly during training.

Observing how the heat affected other athletes, causing them to struggle toward the end of their programs, I focused intensely on the final five elements of my routine. I rehearsed that segment about seven times during the final session, determined not to falter under any circumstances when it counted.

> *Despite Jayson's numerous world medals he had already won, no Australian had ever won the GOLD medal at the world championships. Not until Tammy, of course, the night before. This only ignited Jayson's flame inside him to the next level—a level I had never seen before. Watching him in training, I remember vividly thinking, "If he holds this together, Australia could take out the GOLD in both the ladies and the men's events. Suddenly, it was a real possibility going from no Australian ever having won a gold medal to potentially winning two in the same year... AMANDA BRYANT*

After finishing my training, I returned to the hotel and relaxed, enjoying downtime before a delicious lunch. Surprisingly, back in my room, I fell into a deep and satisfying sleep. I felt remarkably refreshed and invigorated when I woke up—more ready than ever to face the upcoming challenge.

To test my readiness, I sprinted to the pool and jumped in, letting myself sink to the bottom. I lay still on my stomach, holding my breath until it felt almost unbearable. Finally, I pushed off with all my strength, breaking through the surface with a mighty roar and arms outstretched,

JAYSON SUTCLIFFE

> *I wanna win!*

Glancing around to ensure no one had witnessed my spontaneous outburst, I felt a surge of confidence. This declaration was my private motivation, and it fueled my determination. Shaking out my long hair and wiping the water from my face, I basked in the sun's warmth. I was ready. Let's go!

It was time to slip into the puffy silk pleated sleeves I had hand-sewn at Petra's in 1992 once again and fasten the Edwardian-style collar snugly around my neck. Despite the heat, embodying this character was essential. My fingers fumbled with the tiny clasps, and I may have let out a few expletives in frustration, but once they were secure and I was dressed, I took deep, calming breaths.

I drew to skate second last, just before Italian skater Francesco Cerisola, mirroring my draw in 1992—a good omen. This draw allowed me to observe and assess the other competitors' performances before my turn, helping me strategize for a shot at the gold. In theory, it sounded promising, but assumptions are risky. Amanda ran down to greet me and hugged me; I needed it.

> *Come on, Jazzie, you can do this!*

ROLABOI, REVIVAL

As the competition began, I couldn't bring myself to watch anymore. The familiar flutter of nerves returned, and I paced anxiously between the makeshift change rooms. I needed to calm down. Then it struck me—my Walkman. I slipped on the headset and tuned into Kylie Minogue. Her music always lifted my spirits and grounded me. Bopping away to her 1990 hit 'Better the Devil You Know,' I felt pumped and ready to roar again. Thank you, Kylie!

With just three skaters left before my performance, Eric Anderson had already skated, impressively knocking out the short program's winner despite a minor error, opting for a double Lutz instead of a triple. Deep down, I knew he so desperately wanted to win as much as I did, and he now held the top spot, leaving no margin for error on my part. It was now or never.

The moment had arrived. It was the culmination of a childhood dream—to claim the gold medal above all else. For the next few minutes, nothing existed outside of the performance that would secure that coveted gold. Every moment in my life has led to this singular opportunity.

As they called my name, signaling my turn, I glanced at Charmaine for reassurance. She firmly held my hands, silently affirming my readiness. It felt like it was 1990 all over again. With a determined spirit borrowed from Guerra and Cohen's era, I rolled onto the floor, ready to conquer, wearing the costume with the silk pleated sleeves I had made at Petra's house in 1992. It worked perfectly with my routine to the music from 'Interview with the Vampire,' adding an extra layer of drama and flair to the night. Though it felt distant, the crowd erupted in applause as if from another world. I stood poised in my opening stance, perfectly balanced and composed on one foot. The anxiety that had gripped me moments earlier had vanished.

Surrounded by a serene blur of sights and sounds, I immersed myself in the music and the comforting warmth. Not a single negative thought entered my mind as I skated by the judges, lining up for my opening element. My last-minute decision to add the double axel-loop-triple toe loop combination could have easily backfired, but it didn't. Landing the combination, I felt like a thoroughbred racehorse powered by the strength of my childhood cartoon superheroes. Skating past Charmaine, we exchanged a knowing glance as the music intensified, and I nailed the triple flip jump. The exhilaration was indescribable. I knew nothing could stop me now.

With the first three triple jumps executed effortlessly, I had only one remaining element that concerned me—the triple Lutz. As I lined up for the jump midway through the program, I suddenly realized, to my horror, that I was too close to the side barrier. At the last second, in mid-air, I decided to jump a double rotation instead of a triple. Was this a huge mistake? Would it cost me the gold? Panic set in, but only briefly before I dismissed any doubt. I couldn't afford to waver; I needed to commit to the remaining elements precisely as planned.

The rest of my performance was strong, including three more triple jumps. The work I had done in the morning training session on my final block certainly paid off. But I couldn't know if I had performed well enough to medal, let alone steal the gold. But the crowd's roar gave me the sense I had stolen the show. For me, that was enough to an extent.

Charmaine was there to hug me when I came off, exhausted. I sat down with her before the judges unveiled their marks, surrounded by Tammy, Amanda, and Diego. Though it seemed an eternity, only minutes passed before the judges decided.

My scores were high, mostly 9.7 – 9.8, but a few 9.5s appeared in both scores. I couldn't do the mental arithmetic fast enough. Was it silver—again? With no placement revealed until the official results sheet was released, I needed Kristen nearby; she could calculate scores in a second. I knew she would be with her mom, Mary, an avid calculator and devoted supporter, meticulously tallying the numbers at that very moment. I found it interesting that the German judge had scored me the highest. A small part of me wondered if this was because I had supported the German Cup competition earlier in the year. Who knows?

With the uncertainty of the scores, Charmaine sensed my slight disappointment and hugged me tightly. Tammy and Amanda kissed me, genuinely excited about how I had skated. Regardless of the result, I felt proud. I had given it my absolute best, skating my heart out in the intense heat, capping off the year with my personal best. I felt so alive, and it made me understand why I repeatedly put myself through this ordeal. Deep down, I had already won in my own right—that was what truly mattered. Wasn't it?

15

SALTARON LOS CANGUROS

As Charmaine and I left the arena entrance and headed toward the changing room, a small crowd of skaters gathered around us. The passageway was incredibly narrow and packed with officials and athletes, creating significant congestion. I stood close to the wall with Charmaine, reflecting on the recent events. People were hurrying in every direction, like field mice, driven by the urgency of the impending closing ceremony.

Charmaine and I exchanged glances. My eyes welled up with emotion. It was over. Another year of intense work was done. I buried my head in my sweat towel for a moment that felt like an eternity. "Well," I thought,

> *I'll be back next year to take another shot at the gold.*

I knew it wasn't the right time to think about the future. I needed to go with the flow and appreciate what I'd just achieved. I had nothing to lose. Coming into the final in fifth position, any improvement would be a bonus. Even if I didn't win a medal, I'd still be happy. Plus, I could win an overall points medal in the combined event with my figures result, so there was still a carrot dangling in front of me, keeping my hopes high.

I lifted my head, smiled bravely, and stood tall. A distant voice grew clearer and louder. I looked up to see Patrick Venerucci's partner, Cristina Pelli, approaching with a huge grin. She was waving her finger in the air and holding a results sheet. Her petite figure marched hurriedly forward through the busy crowd.

I had no idea what the urgency was about, and I looked around to see if anything was happening around me; there wasn't, so I figured she was coming to tell me I'd moved up into a medal place. As she anxiously pushed through the crowd, she yelled,

> *Number one! … Number one! Jayson, number one!*

My entire body trembled in disbelief as I stared into her eyes. "No way," I gasped. "Are you sure?"

Cristina reached out with both hands, squeezed my cheeks, and kissed me in typical Italian fashion. "Si, si," she cheered excitedly. "Number one." She was shaking, just as I had begun to. It was as if my own mother was breaking the news.

Cristina had the unofficial printout scrunched in her hand. Charmaine grabbed it, glanced, and loudly shrieked when she saw it in black and white. We both stared at each other for a brief second before jumping into each other's arms. Usually composed, Charmaine's uncharacteristic outburst was seriously cool. Everything blurred into a trance-like mist. I wanted to freeze this moment in time for all eternity.

Cristina wrapped her arms around us like a mantle of joy. She knew it had been a long journey to the top, and she had been a friend every step of the way.

Australian team coach and supporter Steve Bowman came to us with the news. He was in tears, repeatedly saying, "You did it, mate. You did it."

I couldn't hug Charmaine hard enough. I didn't know what to do or say. I wanted to cry, scream, and jump up and down madly, yet all I wanted was to call my mom and dad. After a good skate, they were always my first thought, and I knew they'd be anxiously waiting for the result. In this moment of complete ecstasy, it was tough to understand how to respond. One part of me knew I had done it, and the other asked, "What now?" as I stood trembling.

Despite seeing it in black and white print, I wasn't entirely convinced I'd won. The unofficial printout from budding calculators in the stands wasn't always accurate. Then, as Eric Anderson limped slowly toward me, I saw the familiar look of disappointment in his eyes – the look of an athlete who had been ranked second for two years. I felt for him for long seconds until it hit me – if he was that down, I had taken the gold from him. My dream had come true. I was finally, officially, world champion – I'd done it!

Eric didn't need to say anything; we just shook hands. He smiled, and we hugged like good friends do. He was genuinely happy for me, just as I would have been for him. It had been a long battle between us for the past three years, taking turns on the No. 2 and 3 podium blocks, each narrowly missing that elusive number one position that Heath Medeiros deservedly snatched year after year.

Suddenly, I realized I hadn't changed into my Australian Team outfit, and the presentations were about to begin. I raced to the dressing rooms and grabbed my outfit from my bag. Not surprisingly, it was rolled up in a ball. Mom wouldn't have been impressed! For the first time, I was alone. The silence was deafening. I smiled and clenched my fist.

I was reaching for my costume when the changing room door flew open. It was my teammate, Dale Bracegirdle. "You bastard," he said with a smirk. "What?" I gasped.

> *You won the overall combined event as well. You won TWO golds!*

"Bullshit!" I replied. It was too much for me to take in. I needed to sit down briefly, but the presentation was already happening. I had to move—pronto. My hands shook so badly I couldn't lace up my skates properly.

Those few minutes were like a bungee jump, a spontaneous

rush filling my body. Skaters I had known for years from other countries appreciated how hard I'd worked to get here and were eager to congratulate me. I wished so badly that my parents could have been there to relish this incredible moment of pride.

Word spread rapidly, and the entire Australian team soon enveloped me in a cocoon of joyous hugs. It was the final puzzle piece adding to Tammy's glorious victory the night before, and one Australia had been waiting for. It was a moment of triumph that united us all in celebration.

> *In 1991, our family drove to Sydney to watch Jayson compete in the world championships. Due to reasons that a 10-year-old couldn't understand, nor should anyone have to endure, Jayson's skate didn't go as he had hoped. My little heart broke for my idol.*
>
> *However, I soon witnessed him overcome this adversity. Over the next four years, Jay worked tirelessly to achieve his goal.*
>
> *By 1995, it was an immense privilege to be on the Australian team at the World Championships in Colombia and watch his gold medal performance live. He made every member of the Australian team feel like his gold medal belonged to them as well. It was a proud moment I will never forget...*
> *RACHAEL YOUNG (SKETCHER)*

JAYSON SUTCLIFFE

Pride was a feeling that resonated deeply within the entire team, especially our coach, Steve Bowman. Sadly, Steve has since passed away, but this moment meant a lot to him. Despite wearing a neck brace at the time, he didn't let it hinder him from running down the stands to share his joy with us.

> *When it comes to the sport of roller skating, it doesn't matter where you come from in Australia or who coaches you. It's about being an Australian and the landmark achievement of having two world champions in the same event. This was the first time we'd had ever had a world champion in an event, making it monumental for the country to achieve this double award on top of Tammy's win the night before.*
>
> *For Jayson personally, it meant finally reaching a goal he knew was within his grasp. It was his way of saying, 'I have done it, I have done it.' He deserved it more than anyone else I've seen because the passion he had for the sport was immense, and this achievement was a great personal reward for him. It was also a great reward for us because, after years of skating, coaching, and judging, we were all united as a nation. We were there together, and it didn't just feel like Jayson's reward; it felt like our reward too.*
>
> *I was especially impressed with how everyone else reacted. Nations stood up, cheering and applauding, recognizing Jayson's longevity, dedication, and persistence in the sport. He always picked himself up and kept going. Seeing him rewarded at the highest possible level in the world was the greatest feeling for all of us...*
>
> *STEVE BOWMAN (1995 Team Australia Coach).*

Officially, in front of a crowd of thousands, the CIPA President, Mr. Jim Pollard, presented me as the new World Champion. The crowning glory of thirteen years of blood, sweat, and tears—ten years after my first appearance at a World Championships in 1985—was a reality.

Jim had been a big supporter of my involvement in the sport. Year after year, he always greeted me like a long-lost father, inquiring about everything I had been doing. From as early as 1986, when he replied to a letter I sent to the US Federation requesting copies of any Worlds or Nationals videos, he happily sent me the footage along with his best wishes. His unwavering encouragement and genuine interest in my progress significantly impacted my journey.

When I returned to the hotel, I raced to the phone and called my parents. "How'd you go, Jay?" my father calmly asked. "Oh, okay, I guess," I grinned into the phone. I was sitting on my bed with several skaters gathered around, each kicking me for leading my dad on.

I told him I skated well enough to move up from my short program placing and that I got a medal. The others continued to poke at me and mouth silently, "Tell him... tell him." My poor dad sounded unsure how to react.

"Better than last year?" he asked, referring to my third position at the previous world meet.

I couldn't resist any longer.

> *Ummm, hell yes... I WON, I WON, Dad, I WON!!!*

"Yeaaaah?" Dad screamed into the phone from ten thousand miles away. "You bloody ripper," he said, sounding a little overwhelmed, while Mom was naturally in tears, trembling at the sound of my voice. Words failed her, but I knew what she was trying to say. Even though we were so far apart, we were together in a real sense for this moment of joy.

> *When Jayson called us from Colombia, he rang at two o'clock in the morning and just said, 'Oh, so and so came second, and someone else third,' then added, 'But I came first!' He was very excited, and so were we. We yelled out to one another 'He's won!' We were so thrilled and proud... Mom.*

After speaking with Mom and Dad, the hotel phone bill took a real pounding. I called everyone I knew back home in Australia, not always conscious of the time difference and forgetting it was two or three am.

Jonelle Hutchinson, a long-time friend and team coach who was traveling, suggested we call Melissa George. It was a little easier getting in touch with her as she lived in L. A., and the time difference didn't matter so much. It was just as well we called; she, too, screamed with joy when I told her the news.

> *When I moved to the U.S, it really touched me that Jayson called from Colombia to say that he was now the best skater in the world... He'd made it. When I was reminiscing about our days together, it made me a little sad, as so much time has gone by, and the memories I have of Jayson were so important to whom I have become today. All the advice and inspiration showed me that if you work hard and stay focused, you will make it to the top and never change who you are. This may seem contrived, but I stayed so long in roller sports only because of Jayson.*
>
> *Kylie Minogue influenced our lives, and I recall a very vivid moment with Jay during an official training session at a national meeting some years ago. We played her CD loudly, and all the judges frowned at us. They were not impressed. Ironically, only years later, Kylie presented me with the 'Most Popular Actress' award on stage in Sydney at the People's Choice Awards; when embracing Kylie, I remembered how far we had both come...*
> MELISSA GEORGE

Following the excitement of the competition and the presentation of medals, we spent the night back at the hotel, mostly among ourselves, since the other teams were so far away. We were happy to celebrate as a team; after all, Australia was ranked overall No. 2 in the world, defeating the USA for the first time in history, and we had three gold medals to our credit. This also marked the highest national ranking Australia has earned to date. Tammy, Charmaine, and I can always be proud, knowing we made that happen with the team's support.

> *My greatest memories in skating include that incredible night in Bucaramanga when Jayson won two gold medals. It was an unforgettable experience. The atmosphere on the floor and in the stadium was electric, especially after Tammy's win the night before. After the presentations, everyone in the stadium flooded onto the floor, creating a mass of excited and euphoric people.*
>
> *As an Australian, I felt an immense sense of pride, and I believe our team shared that excitement. Winning the second and third gold medals for Australia at that championship was a highlight.*
>
> *I've been to many places and experienced a lot in skating, both before and after that night, but that moment stands out as the pinnacle. And that's my honest opinion...* CHRIS CLOUGH (TEAM MANAGER)

An exhibition gala was planned for the following afternoon, with a rehearsal in the morning that both Tammy and I missed. I didn't have a demonstration planned, so I performed an edited version of my 1994 long program, 'Schindler's List.'

It was the first time I had been introduced onto the skating floor as the world champion—oh, that felt awesome! I trembled as I knelt in my starting position, tasting the salty sweat on my upper lip. It hit me that this was no longer a dream but a reality. Tears filled my eyes during my performance. I felt as though I was skating on air for the first time in my life. As an athlete, I believe this is a once-in-a-lifetime sensation, and this was it for me. At that moment, I didn't just believe in the mythical "cloud nine"; I was on it.

The Colombian Federation had promised the "party of all parties" after the championships. From the sneak peeks we grabbed of the preparations, we had no reason to believe it was an exaggeration—this would be the biggest fiesta the town had ever known. The city center square had been closed off and converted into a giant open-air dining area with seating for over five hundred. Intriguing aromas of local delicacies filled the air, and the streets were lined with hundreds of onlookers behind the roped-off sections.

Traditionally dressed in national costume, waitresses in abundance served 'Fire Vodka' shots to everyone. Thankfully, the team managers overlooked the 'no alcohol' rule stringently applied throughout the championships. It appeared customary that the night should commence with a vodka shot, and who were we to mess with tradition? Charmaine was dressed in a sleek, black, skintight dress with see-through sections that were causing quite a stir, while I sported my black PVC pants and sleeveless shirt with a dinner jacket and sunglasses. I felt like quite the rock star.

ROLABOI, REVIVAL

The townspeople had gone to great lengths to ensure the evening was a success; I had never witnessed, let alone participated in, an "after party" quite like it. However, all the vodka in the world wasn't going to blur the memory of this special night for Tammy and me.

Each year, winners were presented with special awards at the closing dinner banquets of the world championships. This year, finally, it was my turn to stand in front of the crowd and accept the presentation. Tammy and I admired the trophies at the front of the city square, where the presentation table had been set up. They were golden statuettes, each mounted on a marble block, cast in the shape of the town emblem—an ant. It was a unique souvenir, and I was eager to get my hands on mine, but fate had other plans.

After being seated for nearly thirty minutes, hunger and

restlessness began. Suddenly, a thunderous roar from the heavens interrupted the proceedings. Torrential rain poured down in solid sheets onto the crowd below. Mother Nature's wrath unleashed gale-force winds that toppled dinner tables and uprooted umbrellas around the table arrangements. Everyone scattered, seeking shelter as the banquet site turned desolate.

Residents and shop owners swiftly opened their doors, inviting us in with open arms. I dashed into the nearest open door, followed quickly by at least another twenty drenched souls. We sat there, staring at each other in dumbfounded amazement. Still, a little rain (okay, a lot of rain) wouldn't dampen our enthusiasm. I had never seen such a downpour in my life.

Soon, people started playing music, singing, and dancing around the block. I smiled at the total stranger who had become my savior from the storm, leaning out of her front window to spot my teammates. I noticed a few gathered under one of the umbrellas that hadn't blown away, standing in at least a foot of water. It was comical, reminding me of the wetter Melbourne Cup Carnivals. Girls in soaked-through evening dresses ran barefoot, carrying their shoes over their shoulders.

Thirty minutes after it began, the cascading cloudburst disappeared as suddenly as it had arisen. By then, however, most of the food was ruined. We were quickly escorted back to our hotels, but that wouldn't stop us from having one hell of a party. We joined forces with the US team for an impromptu event. The word spread like wildfire almost telepathically, and nearly all the teams had arrived to join together and party.

Neither Tammy nor I received our awards that evening, and not even to this day. However, having the presentation interrupted in such a spectacular fashion only made the whole experience more memorable.

When we finally bid farewell to Colombia, Chris Clough looked like he'd won the lottery. He was now officially the team manager for the most successful Australian Team in history. At the airport, one of the girls from another team approached me and told me I was on the newspaper's front page. I thought she was joking and hurried to the news agency. The headline read 'Saltaron los Canguros' aka 'The Kangaroo has jumped,' accompanied by a full-color photograph of my performance. It was a great honor to be featured, and my first thought was to grab a copy for Mom... one for me... and one for... oh, forget it, how many copies could I carry? I mean, how often does a roller skater get to be front-page news?

I wasn't sure what kind of reception to expect back in Australia. After clearing customs in Sydney and entering the domestic terminal, to my surprise, there was a welcoming party with skaters from clubs around Sydney. It was amazing. This wasn't even my state! Then, I received a message to ensure I wore my Australian tracksuit upon arriving in Melbourne. Initially, I couldn't understand why, but I figured it must have been my mom's idea for some nice photos, so I gladly complied. After such a long trip, none of us were looking or feeling our best.

I couldn't believe my eyes as I walked through the arrival gate in Melbourne. At first glance, I saw my parents and my sister, who had never met me upon arrival, so this was special, with my dad wearing a t-shirt proudly displaying my name and 'Simply the BEST' written in colored glitter! They rushed over to hug me, and Mom, naturally, was in tears. Then, I noticed several banners waving with my name on them. It wasn't until I recognized the Channel Ten News reporter, Charles Slade, that I thought there must have been a sports star or celebrity on the plane. I looked around to see who it might be before realizing the cameraman was headed straight for me!

This was very unusual because our sport doesn't usually receive this kind of attention. Kaye Woodgate, a good friend and mother of two of my former students, Leanne and Samantha, had been busy making calls along with Brad Fraumano to all the networks with the news of Australia's success, and Channel Ten was eager to cover the story on both the 'News' and 'Sports Tonight.' This was the icing on the cake. It was the best promotion a sport could ask for prime-time news with roller sports headlining. As I spoke to the reporter, I could see my parents out of the corner of my eye, glowing like I'd never seen before. Nothing could have made me happier than to see them smiling like that. My interview skills left a lot to be desired, but then again, it wasn't something we were used to. Both my parents put equally as much effort into making me a champion as I had over the years. The triumph was as much theirs as it was mine.

It was hard to come back down to Earth after the spine-tingling experience of the world championships. Did I even want to return to reality? Reality meant decisions. Would I rest on my laurels or defend my title? If I chose to defend my title, I had to start training again almost immediately. Did I really want to go through all of that again? I wasn't ready to give up skating; it wasn't time for that yet. However, I was mentally and physically drained, my body urging me to hang up my skates. Yet, I yearned to prove it wasn't just a stroke of luck. Gold had become like a drug, pulling me back into that competitive arena. I needed to know I could do it again.

I took a brief hiatus before plunging back into training with renewed determination. It was a pivotal moment—a decision that would shape my future. Looking back, I questioned if it was the right choice. As time unfolded, I realized it was a decision I would regret. Yet, always one to follow my instincts, I persevered, embracing the uncertainties of competitive sport with unwavering resolve. This marked the closing chapter of a story filled with challenges, growth, and the unyielding pursuit of my passion—a journey I so desperately wanted to share with those who supported me along the way.

Life in the 21st century has been a whirlwind for many, and mine has been no exception. I've experienced incredible highs and faced daunting lows, shaping a journey that's been nothing short of remarkable. Along the way, I've embraced moments of joy and profound growth that have left a lasting impact. I feel blessed to navigate this path with a clear sense of purpose and gratitude, cherishing each day as an opportunity to connect with others and share in the richness of life's experiences, both on and off roller skates.

At times, my dreams may have seemed disparate, but my belief in the possibility of achieving them remained steadfast in my heart. I carry the wisdom imparted by the influential women in my life—Lynda, Charmaine, and… my mom, in the hope of sharing that with everyone.

'We were all
UNITED
as a
NATION.'

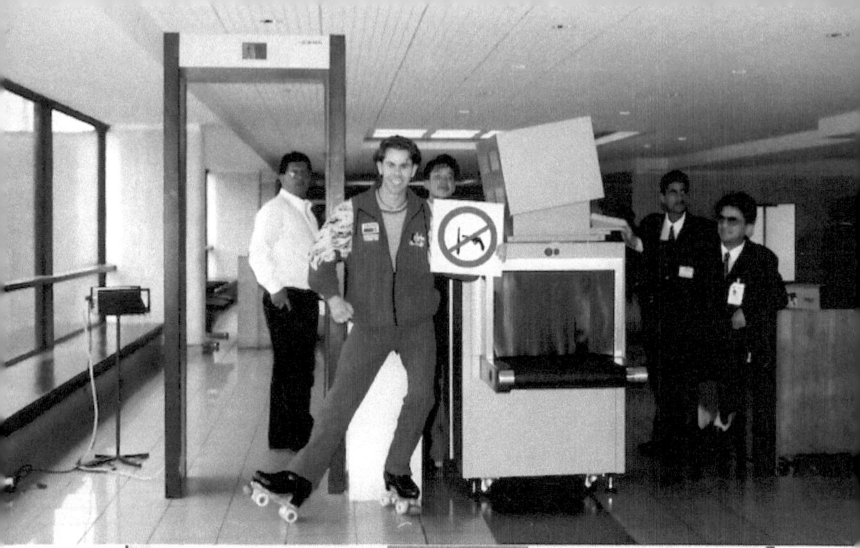

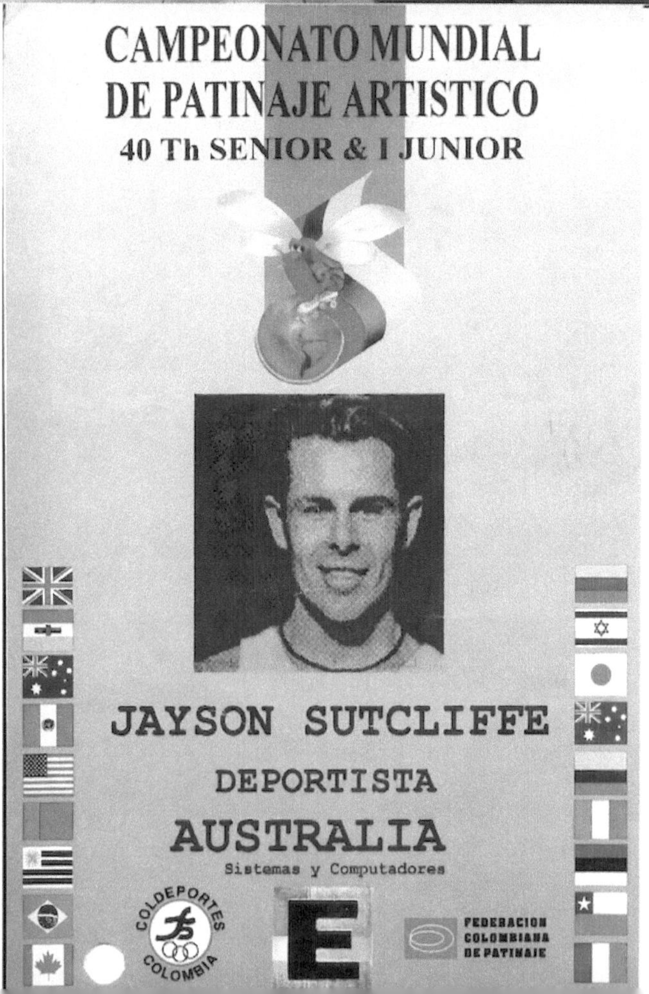
CAMPEONATO MUNDIAL
DE PATINAJE ARTISTICO
40 Th SENIOR & I JUNIOR
JAYSON SUTCLIFFE
DEPORTISTA
AUSTRALIA
Sistemas y Computadores
COLDEPORTES
COLOMBIA
E
FEDERACION
COLOMBIANA
DE PATINAJE

| Director de Coldeportes habla de fútbol y Juegos Nacionales
/ PAG. 6D /  | 1D/ LUNES 4 DE DICIEMBRE DE 1995 SECCION D **Vanguardia Liberal** **Deportes** BUCARAMANGA - COLOMBIA | Bucaramanga em... con Envigado y enfrentará al Pere... /PA... |

Saltaron los canguros

Por JULIO GÓMEZ MORA
VANGUARDIA LIBERAL

El epílogo no fue inferior al desarrollo.

Vaya final que nos tenía preparada la fiesta mu... del patinaje artístico que durante diez días se vivió en Ciudad San Juan Girón.

Se observó el nacimiento de una nueva potenc... Colombia logró la mejor ubicación de toda su historia libre. Argentina, para satisfacción suramericana, volvi... meterse entre los grandes y todo, siempre con el herm... marco de una tribuna completamente llena.

El sábado en la noche, en el cierre de las comp... cias, el australiano Jayson Sutcliffe se consolidó com... gran estrella del patinaje artístico de este planeta.

Dos de oro se colgó el "canguro" al cierre de la j... mación.

Primero, destrozó los pronósticos de la mayorí... el mejor de la modalidad libre; la segunda de oro para... Australia en cuarenta campeonatos mundiales de la c... goría de mayores.

CONTINUA /7...

EL AUSTRALIANO Jayson Sutcliffe, se convirtió en la gran figura de la jornada de cierre del XL Campeonato Mundial de Patinaje Artístico, categoría mayores, al imponerse en las modalidades de libre individual y combinada. De esta forma, el país de los canguros se ubicó en el segundo lugar del medallero con tres de oro, siendo superado únicamente por Italia que acumuló 3 doradas, 2 de plata y 3 de bronce, para un total de 8.

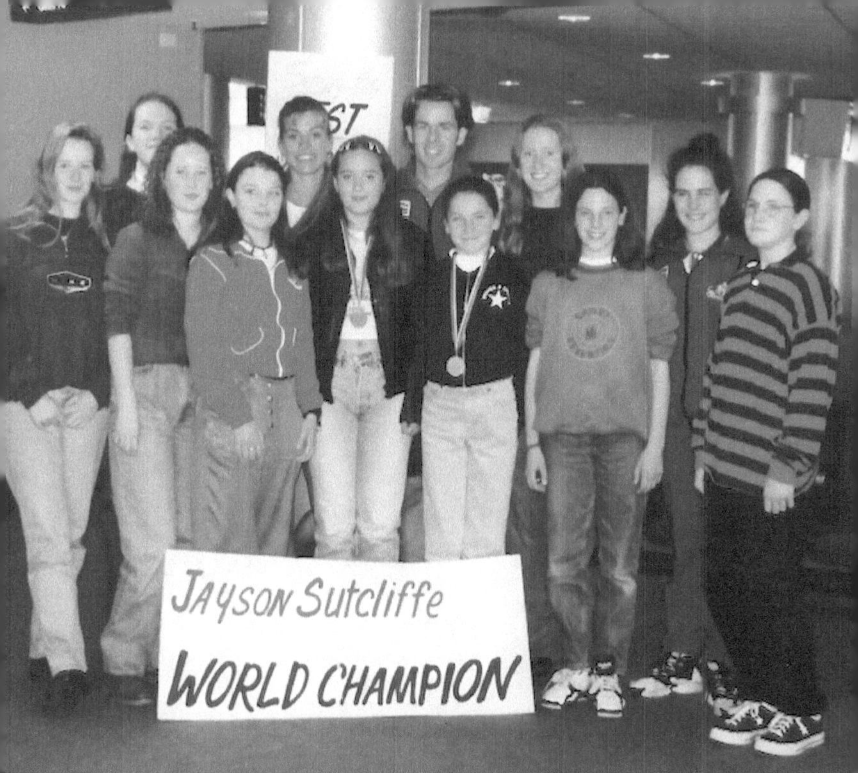
Jayson Sutcliffe
WORLD CHAMPION

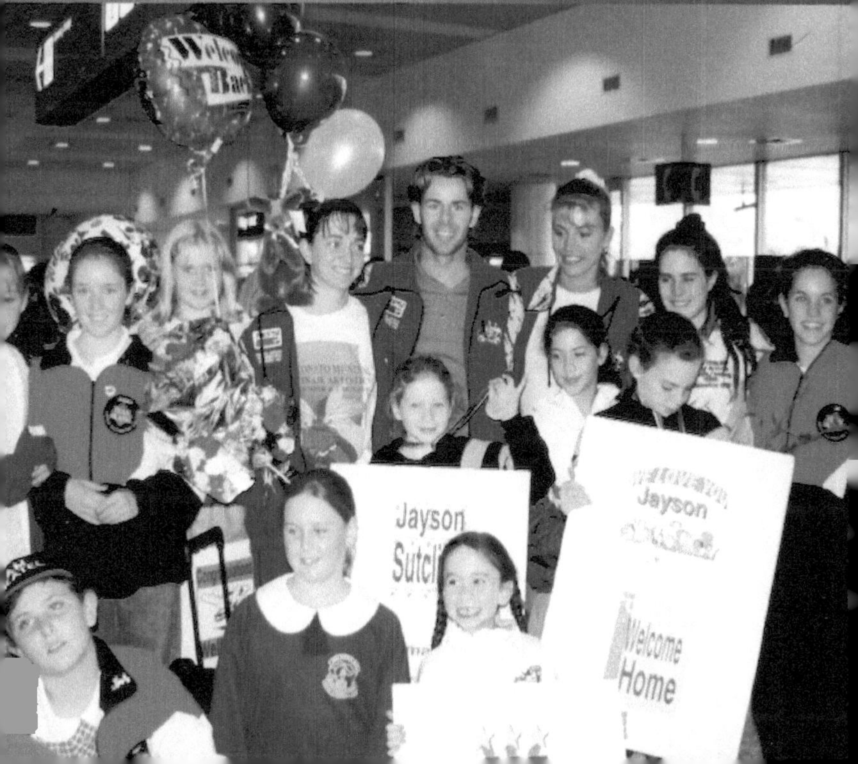
Jayson
Jayson
Welcome
Home

PEPSI

← Exit and baggage claim
← Gates 1-6
Gates 8-12 →
BEST
TAYSON
1
BEST
TAYSON

Senator John Faulkner

Minister for the Environment, Sport and Territories

Mr Jayson Sutcliffe

1 3 DEC 1995

Dear Jayson

I am writing to congratulate you on being the first Australian to win a World Artistic Roller Skating title with your gold medals in the Men's Freeskating and the Men's Combined events at the World Championships in Buccaramanga, Columbia.

It is pleasing to see your hard work and dedication rewarded and I look forward to hearing of your continued success.

Once again, congratulations on a great performance.

Yours sincerely

JOHN FAULKNER

'The Kangaroo has Jumped.'

HISTORY

WORLD CHAMPIONSHIPS (Top 3)

1990 Men's Free Skating - GERMANY, 2nd
1992 Men's Free Skating - U.S.A, 2nd
1993 Men's Overall - FRANCE, 3rd
1993 Men's Free Skating - FRANCE, 3rd
1994 Men's Free Skating - ITALY, 3rd
1994 Men's Overall - ITALY, 3rd
1995 Men's Free Skating - COLOMBIA, 1st
1995 Men's Overall - COLOMBIA, 1st
1996 Men's Overall - ARGENTINA, 3rd
2002 Men's Inline Free Skating - GERMANY, 1st
2003 Men's Inline Free Skating - ARGENTINA, 2nd
2005 Men's Inline Free Skating - ITALY, 1st

WORLD GAMES (all non-Olympic Sports)

1993 Men's Free Skating - NETHERLANDS, 2nd
1989 Men's Free Skating - GERMANY, 5th

HISTORY

GERMAN CUP

1995 Men's Free Skating - GERMANY, 1st
1995 Men's Figures - GERMANY, 3rd
1995 Men's Overall - GERMANY, 2nd

WORLD CHAMPIONSHIPS – Contested

1985, 87-96, 99-00, 02-03, 2005.

HONORS

1991 Sports Star of the Future - The Journal, Dandenong
1993 Sports Star of the Year - The Journal, Dandenong
1996 Hall of Fame - Skate Australia
2002 Life Member - Skate Victoria
2003 Life Member - Caribbean RSC
2006 Sporting Hero Billboard - City Greater Dandenong
2012 Coach of the Year - Skate Australia

AMBASSADOR

2007 World Artistic Roller Skating Championships, AUS

ABOUT THE AUTHOR

Jayson Sutcliffe, hailing from Melbourne, Australia, is a former world champion in roller figure skating. Following his competitive career, he has dedicated most of his life to coaching young skaters and advocating for the sport's growth and awareness globally, including within the LGBTQI community.

His writing journey began in 2001 with the three-year project "Rolaboi, Renegade Skater," released in 2004. He has since pursued writing feature screenplays and TV pilots in the drama genre and coming-of-age journeys.

Additionally, his feature documentary "ROLLERBOY" was a finalist at the 2011 Sydney Film Festival, while his documentary "JESUS CAN'T SKATE" won the Audience Award at the Australian International Film Festival.

Outside of his writing and roller-skating activities, Jayson enjoys visiting cinemas to watch sci-fi and horror films.

For more on Jayson, visit:
jaysonsutcliffe.com

ACKNOWLEDGEMENTS

I have chosen simply to thank everyone. Without omitting any individuals (many of whom have been great friends over the years), I have chosen to thank 'everyone.'

To the many who have supported me tirelessly throughout, without question, and shared their love and friendship... Thank you!

To Melissa George & Luke Dennehy – for your invaluable feedback, testimonials, and kind contributions.

To all the skaters & parents during my competitive years at:

Rollerworld Springvale, Roller City Frankston, Skateworld Noble Park, Dandenong Skate Club, Skate Connection, Springers Leisure Center, The Shed, Jolly Trieste, Ohio Skate, Skateline Modbury, Team Sk8 FX, and Caribbean Rollerama.

To all the coaches and trainers I worked with through to 1995:

Lynda Flint, Charmaine, Simon Reeves, Petra Dayney USA, Peggy Yambor USA, Dennis & Gail Collier USA, Alex Wang TPE, Jocelyn Taylor UK, Mario & Alvia Vitta, and Sandro Guerra ITA.

To the coaches that I've had the pleasure of working with beyond my competitive career:

Linda A'Court (Noble), Cristina Moretti ITA, Gabriele Quirini ITA, Jodie Garufo, Rachael Sketcher, Trace Hansen USA, Jacqui Innes NZ, Vickie Bateman USA, and Tammy Bryant.

To my friends, both here and overseas…
Your kindness, support, and friendship have meant the world to me.

Love to you all.

CONTRIBUTIONS

The following people kindly contributed to my book, making the event more authentic and memorable.

Thank you to each of you:

MELISSA GEORGE
LYNDA FLINT (PAULDING)
AMANDA BRYANT
ERIC ANDERSON
DIEGO FARINA
JACQUI INNES
LIZ INNES
KATHY MASON
JENNY DOWNARD (BEDWELL)
ELIZABETH BOND (VARGA)
APRIL DAYNEY (JACOBSON)
JODIE JOHNSON (GARUFO)
JONELLE HUTCHINSON (McKANE)
RACHAEL YOUNG (SKETCHER)

I would also like to acknowledge the inclusion of the excerpts from interviews conducted for the feature Documentary, 'Rollerboy' courtesy of Circe Films.

COLINE SUTCLIFFE (DAD) R.I.P
BEVERLEY SUTCLIFFE (MOM)
LEANNE SUTCLIFFE (CHRISTIE)
SCOTT COHEN
TAMMY BRYANT
CAROL & JEFF JESSOP
CHRIS CLOUGH
STEVE BOWMAN (R.I.P)

I would also like to acknowledge and thank
LYNN SANTER for her exceptional work as the editor of the 2004 original release of 'Rolaboi, Renegade Skater' through Zeus Publications. Her dedication and expertise were invaluable to the creation of the original edition.

STUDENTS

From 1991 to 2022, I had the privilege of working with many talented skaters, many of whom became lifelong friends. Whether in Australia or around the world, your dedication led many of you to become state, national, and international champions, as well as great role models and strong athletes. I am incredibly proud of each and every one of you.

I extend my sincerest wishes to you and your families for the kindness and support you have always shown. Working with you was always a pleasure, and even in challenging times, we always came together and triumphed. Hardly a day goes by without me reflecting on a moment shared with a skater, remembering our achievements, and the special memories we created.

Continued success and love to you all.

SUPPORT

I would also like to thank the following companies, clubs, and organizations for their continued support during my time as an athlete and coach.

EDEA SKATES
ROLL-LINE
RISPORT
LABEDA USA
CARIBBEAN ROLLERAMA (RSC)
DANDENONG RSC
SKATEWORLD NOBLE PARK
NATIONAL SYSTEMS
SKATE VICTORIA
SKATE AUSTRALIA
FIRS
AUSTRALIAN SPORTS COMMISSION
AUSTRALIAN INSTITUTE OF SPORT
SPORT & RECREATION VICTORIA
VIC SPORT
VIC HEALTH
VICTORIAN INSTITUTE OF SPORT
SK8HOUSE
SKATEAWAY ALBANY CREEK
SKATETRADER, SKATE PARADISE
and SKATE QUEENSLAND.

PHOTOGRAPHIC CONTRIBUTIONS

I would like to extend our deepest gratitude to the following individuals and organizations for their invaluable photographic contributions:

- Sutcliffe family archives
- Carolina (Brante) Heffernan - for taking cover shot.
- Liz Varga, Pg 55 - M.I.A.M.I Seminar SA 84
- Jenny Downward (Bedwell), Pgs 94, 97 - Worlds 85
- Judith Miller (Backway), Pgs 103, 113-116 - EBS
- Elizabeth Varga, Pgs 126, 128 - World Expo 88
- Ian James, Pgs 181, 187-189, Back cover - Hanau 90
- HWT, Pg 190 - 1990 Medalist
- Harry Bracegirldle, Pg 237, 298 - France, Worlds 93
- Dezera Salas, Pg 253, 255 - World Games 1993
- Skate Australia Magazine, Pgs 256, 299
- Harry Bracegirldle, Pg 213, 246, 258 - Sydney, 1991
- Heath Medeiros, Pg 253, Tampa, USA 1992
- Martin Hass, Pg 294, 296 - Italy, Worlds 1994
- Diego Farina, Pgs 329, 363 - Giron, Worlds 1995
- Vanguardia Liberal, Pg 376 - Worlds 1995 Coverage

I want to give special thanks to all the photographers and contributors whose work is featured in this book. Your talent and hard work are greatly appreciated.

I want to extend my sincere gratitude to the creators and rightful owners of the following photographs, many of which have been in my possession for many decades:

- Melissa George, 2003 - Intro
- Jayson, 1985 - Roller City Frankston, Pg 99
- Jayson, Felicity - Skate Connection Hall, Pg 108
- Jayson, 1988 - Pensacola, FL, Worlds, Pg 123
- Jayson, 1990 - Monash Uni, Nationals, Pg 158-159
- Jayson, 1992 - Noble Park Skateworld, Pg 162
- Jayson, 1994 - Brisbane Nationals, Pg 297
- Jayson, 1996 - Adelaide Nationals, Pg 369

Although the sources of these images are unknown, I recognize and appreciate the valuable contributions of the original photographers/publications. If you are the rightful owner of any of these images, please accept our heartfelt thanks and contact me so I can properly credit your work in future editions.

The following images were created using AI.

- Pg 6 - Young boy watching TV
- Pg 9 - Young boy discovering skates

EDITORIAL CONTRIBUTIONS

I would like to extend my sincere gratitude to the creators and rightful owners of the following news articles, which have appeared in the media over the decades and in the RSA (Skate Australia) Annual Magazine:

- Herald Weekly Times Pty Ltd, Herald Sun
- Sporting Images - Duane Hart
- Newspix / Leader
- The Journal, Dandenong
- The Examiner, Dandenong
- Fairfax Regional and Community Newspapers
- Barrier Daily Truth, Broken Hill

- RSA (Skate Australia) Annual Magazine
- Patinaje, FEP, Spain

I recognize and appreciate the valuable contributions of the original photographers/publications. If you are the rightful owner of any of these images, please accept our heartfelt thanks and contact me so I can properly credit your work in future editions.

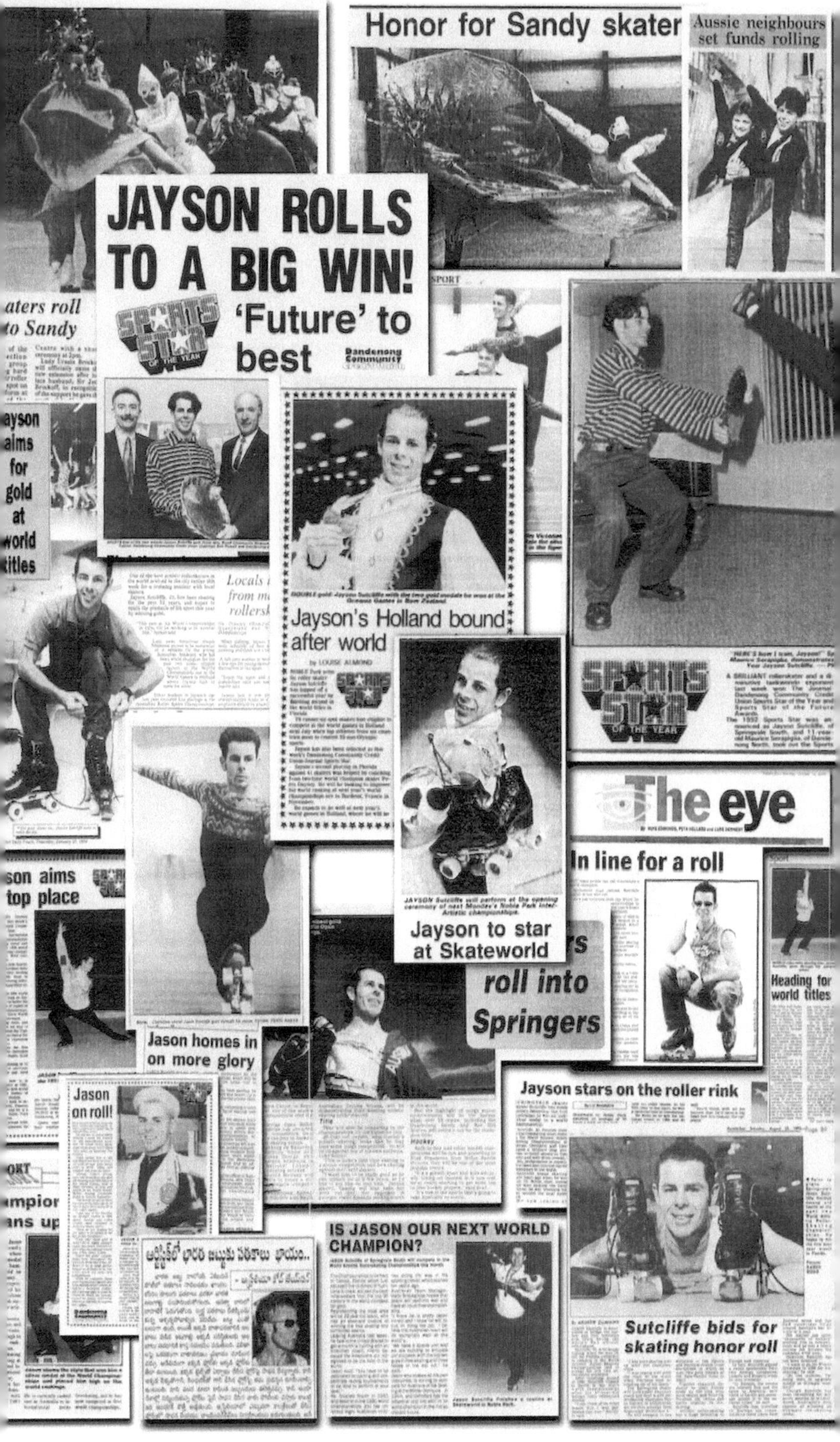

Honor for Sandy skater
Aussie neighbours set funds rolling
JAYSON ROLLS TO A BIG WIN!
'Future' to best
SPORTS STAR OF THE YEAR
Jayson's Holland bound after world
Jayson to star at Skateworld
The eye
In line for a roll
roll into Springers
Heading for world titles
top place
Jason homes in on more glory
Jason on roll!
Jayson stars on the roller rink
IS JASON OUR NEXT WORLD CHAMPION?
Sutcliffe bids for skating honor roll

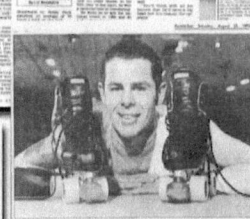

www.ingramcontent.com/pod-product-compliance
Lightning Source LLC
Chambersburg PA
CBHW060547080526
44585CB00013B/469